ISSUE 8, FEBRUARY 2020

AUSTRALIAN FOREIGN AFFAIRS

Contributors

John Blaxland is a professor of security and intelligence studies at the Strategic and Defence Studies Centre at the Australian National University.

Jacinta Carroll is a senior research fellow at the National Security College at the Australian National University.

Helen Clark is a former prime minister of New Zealand.

Christopher Kremmer is a journalism lecturer at the University of New South Wales whose books include *Inhaling the Mahatma*.

Kelly Magsamen is the vice president for national security and international policy at the Center for American Progress and was previously a senior Pentagon and National Security Council official.

Felicity Ruby is a PhD candidate at the University of Sydney who is researching the Five Eyes intelligence alliance.

Brendan Taylor is a professor of strategic studies at the Australian National University.

Michael Wesley is the deputy vice-chancellor international at the University of Melbourne.

Australian Foreign Affairs is published three times a year by Schwartz Books Pty Ltd. Publisher: Morry Schwartz. ISBN 978-1-76064-1771 ISSN 2208-5912 ALL RIGHTS RESERVED. No part of this publication may be reproduced, stored in a retrieval system, or transmitted in any form by any means, electronic, mechanical, photocopying, recording or otherwise, without the prior consent of the publishers. Essays, reviews and correspondence © retained by the authors. Subscriptions – 1 year print & digital auto-renew (3 issues): $49.99 within Australia incl. GST. 1 year print and digital subscription (3 issues): $59.99 within Australia incl. GST. 2 year print & digital (6 issues): $114.99 within Australia incl. GST. 1 year digital only auto-renew: $29.99. Payment may be made by MasterCard, Visa or Amex, or by cheque made out to Schwartz Books Pty Ltd. Payment includes postage and handling. To subscribe, fill out the form inside this issue, subscribe online at www.australianforeignaffairs.com, email subscribe@australianforeignaffairs.com or phone 1800 077 514 / 61 3 9486 0288. Correspondence should be addressed to: The Editor, Australian Foreign Affairs, Level 1, 221 Drummond Street, Carlton VIC 3053 Australia Phone: 61 3 9486 0288 / Fax: 61 3 9486 0244 Email: enquiries@australianforeignaffairs.com Editor: Jonathan Pearlman. Associate Editor: Chris Feik. Consulting Editor: Allan Gyngell. Deputy Editor: Julia Carlomagno. Digital Editor and Marketing: Georgia Mill. Editorial Intern: Lachlan McIntosh. Management: Elisabeth Young. Subscriptions: Iryna Byelyayeva. Publicity: Anna Lensky. Design: Peter Long. Production Coordination: Marilyn de Castro. Typesetting: Akiko Chan. Cover photograph by Newscom/Alamy Stock Photo. Printed in Australia by McPherson's Printing Group.

Editor's Note

CAN WE TRUST AMERICA?

In February 1998, seven years after the Soviet Union collapsed and several months before Google was founded, Madeleine Albright, the US secretary of state, appeared on morning television to discuss recent tensions in Iraq. The United States accounted for 30 per cent of the global economy and 40 per cent of the world's defence spending; the second-biggest military spender was France. "If we have to use force," Albright explained, "it is because we are America."

Famously, Albright then introduced her description of America as "the indispensable nation", a label suggested to her by a White House aide, who had coined it with a historian.

"We are the indispensable nation," Albright said. "We stand tall and we see further than other countries into the future."

Back then, this assertion of unassailability seemed indisputable, not just to viewers of NBC's *The Today Show* but to the international community. Australia, for instance, in its 1997 Foreign Policy White Paper, stated: "The United States will remain, over the next fifteen years, the single most powerful country in the world." In its 2003

Foreign Policy White Paper, it said: "No other country can match the United States' global reach in international affairs."

Albright's comment also contained a presumption – implicit in the tone – that the reason for the United States' indispensable status was not only its contribution to the world's prosperity, security, innovation and culture, but also the superiority of its values and vision.

Today, Albright's truths no longer seem so self-evident. The United States has weathered two inconclusive wars in Iraq and Afghanistan; the global financial crisis has weakened faith in its economic leadership; and partisanship in Washington has paralysed its policymaking. China has emerged as a rising rival power, while Russia and others have tested US power elsewhere.

In 2017, Australia, in its first Foreign Policy White Paper since 2003, claimed: "The United States remains the most powerful country, but its long dominance of the international order is being challenged by other powers. A post–Cold War lull in major power rivalry has ended."

Australia has benefited from the stability in Asia the US presence guaranteed, and from being a staunch ally of the world's unrivalled superpower. Now, in the wake of the post–Cold War lull, Australia will no longer be able to view the alliance as a cosy and ever-dependable security blanket. Washington's demands of Canberra are already changing.

Aside from the emergence of rival powers, other changes have occurred within the United States, where the consensus around its global role appears to be diminishing. Barack Obama and Hillary Clinton used the phrase "indispensable nation"; Donald Trump does not, and nor do several of the front-running Democratic presidential candidates.

The United States' role and self-image may be in flux, yet its power and reach remain immense. It is the world's strongest and wealthiest country. The costs it faces in trying to remain indispensable are growing, but the benefits are no longer guaranteed. So its choices – over its future role in Asia, and its approach to its allies – are becoming less straightforward.

For Australia, this presents serious challenges. It has been able to avoid difficult choices because the US place in the world, and particularly in Asia, was so assured. In this world beyond the lull, Australia will need to understand and anticipate the United States' options and capabilities. This will be crucial if Australia is to maintain confidence in its closest ally, in a region in which a growing number of nations can claim to be indispensable.

Jonathan Pearlman

BEIJING CALLING

How China is testing
the alliance

Michael Wesley

On 20 August 1908, half a million of Sydney's 600,000 people crushed in around the shores of Sydney Harbour. It was the largest public gathering ever in Australia, easily overshadowing the celebrations for Federation seven years before. They were there to see sixteen white battleships of the United States Navy stopping in as part of a global circumnavigation.

Prime minister Alfred Deakin had irritated Australia's imperial ally by directly inviting the US Navy to visit, rather than routing his request through Whitehall. Deakin's letter of invitation to American president Theodore Roosevelt on 7 January 1908 had a strategic motive. Australia was locked into an arrangement to pay £200,000 per year towards the British Navy, yet the portion of the imperial fleet stationed in Australian waters was insignificant and could be withdrawn without consultation.

Even more alarming, Britain had admitted its impotence in the Pacific by forming an alliance with imperial Japan in 1902. To the British government, the alliance made splendid sense: both nations were concerned about Russia, and Japan had modelled its burgeoning navy on Britain's, so Britain felt comfortable subcontracting its imperial interests in the Far East to the Japanese Navy. It was a strategic logic lost on Australians, who were alarmed by Japan's rising power and growing territorial demands. By subcontracting the defence of the Empire's Pacific territories to Japan, Deakin thought, the British government had given the fox responsibility for the henhouse. He wanted to build Australia's own navy and thought that a visit by a powerful American flotilla may embarrass Whitehall into accepting his case.

Australians christened the American visitors "the Great White Fleet" in a surge of pride at what their Anglo-Saxon kin on the other side of the Pacific could achieve. But amid the celebrations of fraternity in Sydney, Melbourne and Albany, the officers of the Great White Fleet were quietly collecting intelligence on Australia's coastal defences. These reports contributed to an American plan to attack British Pacific bases, including in Sydney, Melbourne, Perth, Fremantle, Albany and Auckland, should Britain's alliance with Japan draw it into a war between the United States and Japan in Asia.

Ironically, in this episode of naivety and deception lies the origins of Australia's defence alliance with the United States. Historical accounts of its birth focus on an 837-word treaty signed at San Francisco on 1 September 1951. Sentimental accounts focus on the

Battle of Hamel in July 1918, where Australian and American troops first fought side by side under General Monash. But the alliance's geopolitical essence has its origins in the steady alignment of Australian and American strategic interests in the Pacific as British power waned and Japanese influence grew. The Great White Fleet's visit in 1908 was Australia's first, semi-conscious admission that it could no longer rely on British protection against a hostile power, and that only the United States was capable of enforcing a regional order Australians could live with.

In 1925, Australian prime minister Stanley Melbourne Bruce again invited a US Navy fleet to visit Australian ports. This time, the Americans sent fifty-six battleships.

Access to Asian markets has underpinned much of Australia's post-Empire prosperity

The challenge of Asia and the birth of a treaty

Australia and the United States share the same strategic imperatives. Historically, each nation has sought absolute security by dominating its landmass and securing its ocean approaches. But the geography of the Pacific makes safeguarding these maritime approaches difficult. Unlike the Atlantic or Indian oceans, the Pacific hosts a continuous girdle of islands along its western shores, running from the Aleutians in the north, through Japan, Taiwan, the Philippines, Indonesia and Australia, to Polynesia in the south. Islands are potential bases from which military power can be projected, by missiles and aircraft as surely as by wooden sailing ships. Despite the vastness of the Pacific, American and Australian strategists have remained preoccupied with the vulnerabilities and opportunities presented by this huge island chain.

At the same time, and despite their wariness of Asia in security terms, both America and Australia have been inexorably drawn towards Asia by their commercial interests. American traders took advantage of the Napoleonic Wars to build trans-Pacific trade in the late eighteenth century. The profits they made transformed Boston, New York and Philadelphia into glittering metropolises and financed the growth of America's first giant companies and banks. As its power grew, the United States did not seek its imperial sphere in Asia, but equal access to all spheres. From Matthew Perry's Black Ships entering Tokyo Bay to John Hay's Open Door Policy advocating China's territorial integrity along with commercial access for all, the ability to prosper from the economic potential of Asia has been a strategic priority for the United States.

Asian demand for Australian products has been a confounding challenge to Australia's Empire loyalties since before Federation. Trade underpinned its rapid rapprochement with its wartime enemy Japan. Later, even as it refused to recognise communist China, its wheat sales to the People's Republic grew stubbornly. Access to Asian markets has underpinned much of Australia's post-Empire prosperity.

But these commercial opportunities carry a hidden cost, altering regional power dynamics. The challenge, for the United States and Australia alike, has been how to maximise the economic benefits of engagement with Asia while forestalling the geopolitical consequences of the region's vitality and growth. The priorities for both countries are maintaining commercial access and political influence in Asia; keeping the great Pacific archipelago in friendly, or at least neutral, hands; and preventing regional domination by a hostile power that could use Asia's resources to menace North America and Australia. But while their imperatives align, the two nations' capabilities do not. The United States has ample power but lacks proximity to Asia; Australia has proximity but lacks the power to shape regional outcomes. Both countries seek to influence the continental and archipelagic orders from afar, but with different advantages and disadvantages. In the alignment of strategic priorities, and in the complementarity of geography and capabilities, lies the geopolitical essence of the Australia–United States alliance.

The alliance has evolved in response to changing imperatives in Asia. What brought Australia and the United States together, long before a formal treaty was signed, was Japan's mounting power and aspirations in Asia. The steady growth of its control over North-East Asia between the 1890s and 1945 translated into island bases in Taiwan, and in the Ryukyu, Marshall and Caroline island groups. Its thirst for markets and raw materials led to invasions of Manchuria and China, and designs on British, French and Dutch colonies in

South-East Asia. As it seized European and American colonies, Japan promoted an anti-Western nationalism within an exclusive, imperialist Greater East Asia Co-Prosperity Sphere.

Meanwhile, Japan's army and navy raced down the island chain, invading New Guinea and Solomon Islands in 1941, within weeks of the attack on Pearl Harbor. For Australians, the folly of relying on the British Empire for protection became manifest. Hong Kong and Singapore capitulated, with 15,000 Australian soldiers captured. As Australia's northern cities were bombed, most of its armed forces were fighting in the Mediterranean. The war in Europe was given priority over the Pacific conflict, and it was only through open defiance of British strategy that prime minister John Curtin brought Australian troops back to New Guinea. As Australians fought a vicious jungle war against the Japanese, the British and Americans blithely planned the postwar order in the Pacific at a summit in Cairo. Australian and American forces regrouped in Australia, and soon the archipelago that had enabled a lightning Japanese advance became its vulnerability as American forces leapfrogged fortified islands and advanced towards Japan, leaving thousands of imperial troops marooned behind the battlefront. As Japan's soldiers retreated or surrendered, they left in their wake a virulent revolutionary nationalism that would see China, northern Korea and northern Vietnam install communist regimes, and anti-colonial struggles break out elsewhere.

The impetus to formalise the wartime partnership flowed from the experience of the Pacific War. For the United States, the brutality of the battles for Guadalcanal, Saipan and Iwo Jima led to a resolve to never again allow hostile interests a foothold in the Western Pacific. Its postwar planning included securing island bases along the archipelago, an early opportunity for Canberra to suggest a formal security partnership. The war had underlined for Australia the advantages of reliance on a friendly resident power rather than a declining, distracted and disintegrating Empire. It had also demonstrated the dangers of an unequal partnership. Great powers – even dear old Blighty – were haughty and selfish, prone to casually assuming the support of the colonies and smaller allies while refusing them input into strategy. Now, even as the dust settled after the Pacific War, Britain wanted

The ANZUS Treaty was almost studied in its vagueness

Australian troops to return to the Middle East to guard against a communist thrust there, while the United States wanted Australia to agree to the rehabilitation and reconstruction of Japan. Foreign minister Percy Spender's price was a formal American security guarantee and access to the highest levels of Western strategic planning within the NATO alliance.

Australia got neither. The Australia, New Zealand and United States (ANZUS) Treaty binds its signatories to three commitments: to work together to strengthen their military capabilities, to consult on threats in the Pacific and to meet common dangers as their constitutions permit. No NATO-like joint command structure or shared planning process; no an-attack-on-one-is-an-attack-on-all commitment; no collective regional security guarantee. Nor was there any formal connection to NATO or to other American security commitments in the Pacific. The ANZUS Treaty was almost studied in its vagueness, reflecting Washington's reluctance to provide carte blanche security guarantees to small and isolated allies that had yet to prove they wouldn't drag America into their own local squabbles. But Australia agreed to the treaty, to taking part in a global containment of communism and to a non-punitive peace treaty with Japan, thanks to a quiet confidence that shared interests in Asia would allow it to build a more intimate partnership with the United States.

This was not a deluded position. The treaty had been preceded by the establishment of joint planning on maritime strategy between the three ANZUS allies. The March 1951 Radford-Collins Agreement committed Australia, New Zealand and the United States to the collective management of sea lanes in the Eastern Indian Ocean and the Western Pacific. By the time the ANZUS Treaty was signed, Australia was also part of America's most intimate intelligence-sharing arrangement. The 1948 UKUSA Agreement designated Australia and New Zealand, along with Canada, as second parties to an arrangement with the United States and Britain to share signals intelligence, and to divide the world into spheres of responsibility for collecting that intelligence. America's and Britain's NATO allies were given much lower levels of access and responsibility. Within five years of the ANZUS Treaty's signing, growing instability in South-East Asia led to five-power consultations among the three ANZUS allies and Britain and France. This gave Australia access to the strategic thinking of NATO's three most powerful members.

The challenge of Asia began to evolve, giving depth and substance to the alliance that the Treaty had not. By the 1950s communism was pushing forward in Asia more powerfully than in any other region, backed by an alarming alignment between China and the Soviet Union. For Australians, the prospect of a rerun of 1942, with Soviet-armed People's Liberation Army troops taking the place of Imperial Japanese Forces, seemed all too real. In a conversation with US president Dwight Eisenhower in the Oval Office, Australian prime minister Robert Menzies sketched out a scenario describing the advance of communist control through South-East Asia that would become popularised as the domino theory. Australia committed forces to help Britain defend Malaya against communist subversion and Indonesian irredentism, and then sent troops to help America defend South Vietnam.

But as military historian Peter Dean observes, the world wars had changed the way Australia contributed to allied operations. There would no longer be major commitments of forces to coalition operations; Australia would deploy highly effective, niche capabilities on its own terms. It would gain maximum alliance advantage, and a right to be consulted, at a much smaller risk. The focus of Australia's approach was to gain status as a significant American ally by virtue of its distinctive contributions to the United States' global capabilities and Pacific strategy. Central to this was its agreement to host American intelligence facilities on Australian soil. The base at North West Cape in Western Australia was crucial to supporting the US sea-based nuclear deterrent against the Soviet Union; Pine Gap in the Northern Territory to controlling US geostationary satellites; and Nurrungar in South Australia to supporting Eastern Hemisphere satellites.

Australia shifts from ally to "mate"

In the 1960s, the challenge of Asia shifted again. The communist monolith that a decade earlier seemed poised to dominate Eurasia dissolved into bitter hostility and open conflict between China and the Soviet Union. US president Richard Nixon announced what would become the Nixon Doctrine, warning America's allies that Washington would help them against an all-out communist assault but not with lower-level defence contingencies. He also embarked on a rapprochement with China, the fomenter of lower-level communist subversion in South-East Asia.

In 1972, a new Labor government had anticipated an Asia no longer riven by Cold War confrontation and realised that, as it tried to build partnerships with its non-aligned neighbours, being too closely associated with the United States could be a foreign policy liability. It also realised that making niche contributions to allied expeditionary campaigns in Asia suited neither Australia's defence interests nor America's post-Vietnam aversion to fighting in Asia.

A cognitive shift in Australia's thinking about the alliance had begun less than ten years after the ANZUS Treaty's signature, even though the full policy framework would not emerge until the 1980s. Canberra's strategic planners grasped that while Australia and the United States would more often than not agree on the big-picture challenge of Asia, they could well disagree on more local contests. It was a question of how geography influenced each ally's perspective. Mighty and distant, the United States had the luxury of focusing on the great-power balance in Asia, interpreting everything through that lens. Weaker and closer to Asia, Australia would evaluate regional

It seemed history had ended, taking the challenge of Asia with it

contingencies through the prism of its own vulnerabilities. When Indonesian president Sukarno proclaimed an objective of *Indonesia Raya* – "greater Indonesia" – Washington saw a potential counterweight to the Sino–Soviet behemoth. Canberra saw an unstable, aggressive nationalist power that could threaten its mandate territory in Papua New Guinea and menace its sea lanes.

The alliance would always be triggered in the case of a major attack on Australia, because a hostile great power would almost certainly already be in confrontation with the United States. But if Australia's relations with its immediate neighbours became fractious, it was more than possible that the United States would resist being drawn in to any resulting conflict. The posture of self-reliance within the alliance followed: Australia, supported by American intelligence and technology, had to be capable of both defeating an attack from its immediate neighbours and fighting in coalition with the United States against major aggression in Asia.

This posture allowed the Labor government, led by Bob Hawke, to stare down its pacifist wing, arguing that the alliance underpinned Australia's sovereignty and independence while American intelligence bases on Australian soil buttressed global nuclear deterrence. Hawke commissioned a review of the alliance in 1983, during his first months in office. It affirmed his position, reporting that, despite the ANZUS Treaty's ambiguities, it brought substantial deterrence and intelligence benefits.

Meanwhile, New Zealand's Labour government became caught on the other side of the sovereignty briar patch, rejecting visits to port by nuclear-armed or -powered US Navy vessels, and was summarily ejected from the alliance in 1986.

With Australia's strategy of self-reliance within a broader framework of reassurance, Hawke achieved greater flexibility in an Asia that had moved on from Cold War rivalries. Australia shifted its foreign policy approach. Working with Japan and Indonesia, it promoted new regional institutions to ensure its access and influence, to focus on economic cooperation and to help socialise former Cold War foes into habits of stability and prosperity. The United States, worried that the new regionalism would weaken its alliances and leave it on the outer, lobbied successfully to join the emerging institutions, while moving to strengthen its alliances with Japan, Korea and Australia. The 1996 Sydney Statement, signed at a meeting of foreign and defence ministers, began a process of deepening the interoperability of Australian and US forces and making Australian territory available for US military training and basing. The closer links, in turn, gave America's allies the confidence to engage deeply with China, once the target of their fear and loathing.

It seemed history had ended, taking the challenge of Asia with it. Supporters of the alliance began to worry that the generations of Australians and Americans who had fought side by side in the Pacific, Korea and Vietnam would pass on, leaving the alliance without a constituency. Harvard political scientist Samuel Huntington labelled Australia a "torn country", determined to jettison its Western identity and merge with Asia. University centres and a leadership dialogue were established to foster mutual understanding between Australia and the United States.

Then, out of a clear morning, hijackers crashed two passenger jets into the World Trade Center in New York and another into the Pentagon in Washington, killing 3000 Americans. Prime minister John Howard was in Washington, and witnessed first-hand a sense of public shock and outrage even greater than that after the attack on Pearl Harbor. On his way home, Howard invoked Article V of the ANZUS Treaty, which covers "an armed attack on the metropolitan territory of any of the Parties". Australia quickly made its trademark potent but niche contribution to the US invasion of Afghanistan, from where the attacks had been planned, and later to the controversial invasion of Iraq. Australian and American troops have since been deployed together in the Middle East for longer than their collaborations in the world wars, Korea and Vietnam combined. An unprecedented level of interoperability, embedding of personnel, intelligence sharing and political intimacy has followed. The language and focus of the alliance has changed.

US leaders habitually talk about their alliances in terms of their country's foundational ideals, in language that often used to ring hollow to pragmatic Australian ears. Yet as historian James Curran notes, from the late 1990s Australian leaders began to speak about the alliance in similarly idealistic terms. Shared democratic values replaced convergent interests as the rationale for an increasingly intimate partnership. At the same time, the domestic politics of the alliance shifted. Polling showed around eight in ten Australians supported the alliance, even as huge crowds marched in Australian streets to protest against involvement in the Iraq War.

In 2004, an Opposition attempt to make political capital by criticising the government's closeness to the United States ended in decisive electoral defeat. Ever since, no politician in either major party would risk questioning the alliance, or even reviewing it, as Hawke did in 1983. For both sides of politics it became values, not interests, that had led Australians and Americans to fight shoulder-to-shoulder from one end of Eurasia to the other. Today, this narrative has morphed into a slick marketing campaign celebrating more than a century of "mateship" in fighting the enemies of freedom together. It occludes the true history of the partnership, ignoring the complementarities and disagreements, the strategic calculations and limited liability commitments, in favour of a chronicle of mutual loyalty, ideological solidarity and undying fealty.

How China complicates the alliance

The challenge of Asia has not disappeared, any more than history has ended. In 1978, China abandoned its role as the epicentre of world revolution and embarked

China is impinging on Australia's sense of security in ever more pressing ways

on emulating the great powers that had brought it, humiliatingly, to its knees. It took just over two decades for China's economy to eclipse all others in trade and manufacturing, and all except the United States' in absolute size. It joined regional institutions warily, fearing America and its allies would dictate proceedings and force their preferences, but soon found institutions such as Asia-Pacific Economic Cooperation (APEC) highly effective in helping to sell reassuring messages about the benefits of engaging with its booming economy.

Yet rather than accepting a role akin to Japan's – economically successful but unthreatening to the American-led system of alliances and free trade – China engaged in regular confrontations with the United States and its Pacific allies from the mid-1990s. Its military scale-up was aimed at removing the US Navy's freedom to impose stability in the Western Pacific without contest. Beijing targeted aircraft carrier battle groups – the key to America's ability to project power across the Earth's largest ocean – with interlocking systems involving hypersonic missiles, seabed sensors, anti-satellite missiles and submarines, creating the most dangerous operating environment the US Navy had faced since 1942.

China also began a campaign to break US alliances, using its status as the number-one trading partner for most Asia-Pacific economies to induce greater independence from Washington. Between 2012 and 2016, Beijing embarked on a series of chess-like moves in the South China Sea and the East China Sea designed to raise doubts about the United States' credibility as an ally. In 2012, Washington's refusal to court conflict to protect Philippines territorial waters from a Chinese claim sent a shiver through the region; in 2014, its backing of Japan in a similar dispute had only a partially calming effect.

While China's combination of statecraft and swagger has not dismantled any significant alliances, its long-term challenge to US power in the region has had profound consequences. President Obama's announcement of a "pivot" to the Pacific, delivered in a speech to the Australian parliament in 2011, had the opposite of its intended effect, as regional governments questioned privately and publicly whether the United States even had the capacity to stare down China's challenge. In the face of China's rise, the United States has relied more on its allies, as well as other regional powers such as India and Vietnam, for ballast in its response to China, at a time when each of these powers harbours growing doubts about US capacity and resolve. This is the case even in Australia, the ally that has drawn closest to the United States over the last quarter-century. Despite the rhetoric of convergent values and unprecedented intimacy, Canberra has spent much of the past decade quietly building its defence relationships with other Asian states, such as Singapore and Japan, which share anxieties about China's growing influence. Its championing of the term "Indo-Pacific" in its most recent Defence and Foreign Policy white papers is code for the hope that India will play a role in balancing China's rise.

Not so long ago, Australia's leaders spoke confidently of not having to choose between the United States and China. But the national mood on China has shifted sharply. Now there is a pervasive dread over almost every strand of our engagement with China, revealing a sense of vulnerability deeper and broader than at any time in our history. China is impinging on Australia's sense of security in ever more pressing ways. As strategist Paul Dibb has pointed out, China's bases in the South China Sea have put Australia within bombing range of potentially hostile forces for the first time since the Pacific War. Its attempts to lease an entire island in Solomon Islands raises fears of hostile bases just off Queensland's coast. Australia has gravitated closer to the United States, yet the alliance no longer provides us with the assurance and confidence in dealing with China it once did. This coincides with a US president who is openly disparaging of allies and willing to engage with rivals and rogue states. Even as Australia's neighbours have transcended their internal instabilities to begin investing heavily in their defence, Australia has been spending lavishly on its internal security and defence while running down its diplomatic resources and slashing its aid budget.

Donald Trump has jettisoned his predecessors' careful approach of balancing economics with geopolitics in relation to China. As the United States abandons all hope of a liberalised China, and embarks on decoupling its innovation and technology sectors from the nation, Trump has set the course towards confrontation. But he is not entirely retreating from Asia, where America has much to gain, and too much to lose if it simply withdraws. Asia will become more and more important to the US economy. Trump is trying to establish a more sustainable domestic political basis for an ongoing role in the Pacific, seeking to force allies to pay more for their defence collaborations and to reduce US trade deficits to counter perceptions that Washington is being exploited.

And the United States is looking to return to its traditional strategy in Asia: not seeking supremacy, but rather to deny it to any other power. The Pentagon and Washington's think tanks are discussing how to counter China's threat to the forward presence of the US Navy. The United States is looking to disperse bases across the Indo-Pacific in places such as Singapore, Australia and the island of Diego Garcia, and to use missiles and submarines to threaten Chinese operations, just as China menaces US capabilities in the region. Australia is vital to this new approach, providing both depth and distance to efforts to deny China control over the Western Pacific. Australia's geography has assumed greater importance in US calculations, and it has therefore become of greater interest to China.

The challenge of Asia has in fact returned in emphatic form. China has a capacity to directly threaten Australia and the United States, as well as setting the terms of their engagement with, or disengagement from, Asia. Beijing's forms of leverage vary, and its intentions are opaque. The states of the Pacific archipelago between China and Australia

As the United States needs Australia more, we have the chance to shape the alliance in our interests

sit uncertainly on a spectrum between alarm and pragmatism in relation to the rise of China, worried about Beijing's intentions but accepting the need to build sustainable relationships with it. Several of these nations are politically unstable and open to external influence, and orientation towards Beijing is becoming a key schism in domestic politics. Adding to the uncertainty is a US president who has made unpredictability central to his approach to international affairs. All of these factors make a sudden realignment of regional relations entirely possible. In short order, Australia and the United States could find Asia dominated by an antagonistic great power, to which the region aligns strategically and economically, leaving them without commercial or diplomatic access and influence – the shared interests that have been the bedrock of the alliance.

This scale of challenge tests the alliance as never before. The United States now expects more of Australia, not in the Middle East but in its backyard. Washington is not pondering whether to ask to use our soil for bases and missile batteries, but when and how. Until now, Australia has hosted joint intelligence facilities but not US bases; allowing the United States to operate bombers and missiles from Australian soil would knit us more tightly to US strategy in Asia. This, along with deepening interoperability of Australian and US forces, would remove much of the discretion the ANZUS Treaty permits.

The building of US bases and missile defence systems has made domestic politics in Europe, Japan and South Korea highly volatile, and can be expected to do the same in Australia. And as the United States has become more reliant on Australia as an ally, we should worry that an increasingly confrontational America will provoke a conflict with China that is not in Australia's or its neighbours' interests.

Yet Australia's continual invoking of loyalty and sacrifice has given the alliance a marriage-like status, in which adherence to our ally's cause has become a test of national character. We have lost sight of the limited-liability nature of the alliance at a time when this quality is more necessary than ever. As the United States needs Australia more, we have the chance – and the obligation – to shape the alliance in our interests. Instead, we have become less questioning and more compliant with each presidential tweet.

The future of the alliance

So how should we shape the alliance? Primarily, we should seek to make it less about fighting a seemingly inevitable war and more about preventing an entirely avoidable one. As Sino–American rivalry deepens, the weight of our attention is on our alliance obligations in the event of war. We forget that the primary reason for alliances is to prevent wars. In the fervid dread about China, the challenge of Asia has dragged Australia and the United States into a military mindset, to the detriment of the diplomatic and developmental arms of their statecraft.

No doubt a clever military strategy will be necessary to prevent China from dominating the region, but it will not be sufficient. We must deploy the other arms of our statecraft to build a set of institutions and norms to stabilise a contested power order, or the region will become increasingly prone to conflict.

In the midst of the Cold War, NATO and the Warsaw Pact saw the development of a set of crisis-management protocols, as well as the Helsinki Process, which stabilised a highly volatile set of relationships. While military forces remained at the ready on both sides, diplomacy and aid did the work that ensured these forces did not see action.

The new challenge of Asia for Australia and the United States is not military but diplomatic and developmental. China is wealthy and powerful, but this does not make its domination of Asia inevitable, or guarantee that other countries in the region will orient themselves towards it. The Australia–US goal in Asia is to convince China's neighbours that it is possible to retain their strategic independence even as they remain tied economically to the region's largest economy. To do this, we need a greater investment in diplomacy and development assistance, not cuts to these resources. Australia has a position of influence with the United States as never before, and it should use it to turn the alliance into a diplomatic tool for bringing stability and balance to Asia. For seventy years Australia has been creative in reshaping its alliance with the United States around the evolution of their shared challenges; it must rediscover this tradition at a time of arguably the greatest contest over their positions in Asia. ■

SILENT PARTNERS

US bases in Australia

Felicity Ruby

Pine Gap wasn't on the agenda at the state dinner in the White House Rose Garden, but the most valuable asset in the US–Australia defence alliance was busy, as ever. Only hours before Prime Minister Scott Morrison and President Donald Trump tucked into their Dover sole with parsley crisps, the base had almost certainly helped aim the drone that mistook Afghan pine-nut farmers for Islamic State fighters. Thirty civilians resting after a day in the field in Nangarhar Province were killed, and forty others were injured.

At the pre-dinner press conference, Trump referred to the upgraded US nuclear arsenal as being in "tippy-top shape". This category of indiscriminate weapons relies on Pine Gap to assist with aiming at targets and to seek, locate and jam, evade or destroy air defence radars. Presumably, the statement Morrison made about the alliance upon arrival in the United States – both nations "see the world through the same eyes", he claimed – was not intended to be taken literally. Yet this comment correctly describes the combined infrastructure and surveillance facilities of the Five Eyes, the signals intelligence-gathering alliance established in 1947 between the United Kingdom, the United States, Canada, Australia and New Zealand. For decades, successive Australian governments have kept the operations of the network secret. Much of what is known about it was revealed by the US National Security Agency (NSA) whistleblower Edward Snowden, whose memoir was released earlier that week.

This example from a week in the life of Pine Gap underscores its role in anchoring the US–Australia defence alliance. Since the signing of the ANZUS Treaty in 1951, Australian governments have relied on the United States to assist if our security is seriously threatened, and they have banked on US dependence on bases such as Pine Gap to help lock in this guarantee. Yet there is very little public understanding or discussion of these bases, or their uses, or the way in which they have constrained Australian foreign policy. This is because successive governments have tried to ensure that they remain clandestine, extending the legitimate need for some operational secrecy to almost blanket silence. Yet the Australian government is aware of, and concurs with, activities at bases such as Pine Gap, which supports the United States' day-to-day combat operations, planning for nuclear war and ongoing surveillance and intelligence-gathering activities. Pine Gap is also used for extrajudicial assassinations, which have killed countless civilians in addition to those deemed terrorists – a function that exposes Australia to possible retribution and our military personnel to litigation.

Snowden's leaks have led to greater discussion in the Australian media, in parliament and among social movements about the very existence of facilities such as Pine Gap and the Five Eyes arrangement of which it is part. Five Eyes was not mentioned in an Australian Defence White Paper until 2016, in a paragraph that also discussed Pine Gap. Since Snowden, Australian officials have moved from "neither confirming nor denying" the existence of Five Eyes to casual mentions of it, and more recently to media and public relations efforts before and after Five Eyes gatherings. But there has been little public consideration of the benefits of this shadow foreign policy, or of the costs of the US surveillance and military bases in Australia. At a time when faith in the rules-based international order and trust in the United States' willingness and capacity to exercise global leadership is decreasing, Australians need to understand the functions of Pine Gap and similar facilities and to evaluate the role they play in the nation's defences, foreign policy and international standing.

> **Tanter asserts, "Pine Gap is perhaps the most important United States intelligence facility outside that country"**

An island with aerials

Over the last forty years, much of the public information about the facilities that underpin the US–Australia alliance emerged from the research of Desmond Ball, a former academic at the Australian

National University who died in 2016. Working with colleagues to sleuth and sift through the public documentation available from the more-forthcoming US freedom of information system and congressional processes, Ball explained the evolution of the political cooperation that led to the development of joint military facilities. He explored the functions of these facilities, and the policy consequences for Australia of being embedded within the military strategy of another nation. Large sections of his books are pretty hard work due to swathes of technical detail and military acronyms, but he detailed painstakingly how Australia is tied into US nuclear war planning, verification of arms control agreements, and ongoing military and surveillance operations and joint exercises.

For his work in publishing and updating centralised repositories of data on the most secret alliance facilities in Australia, Ball earned a two-volume ASIO file now housed in the National Archive. Apparently Sir Arthur Tange, defence secretary throughout the 1970s, considered Ball to be "aiding the enemy". Former defence intelligence official Paul Dibb believed the department's obsession with Ball was a form of paranoia, making the accolades at Ball's memorial from defence officials and former ministers all the more excruciating.

Ball's 1980 text, *A Suitable Piece of Real Estate*, published at the height of the Cold War, discussed frankly the likelihood of US bases in Australia being nuclear targets, and predicted the types of information US satellites would beam down to be collected at these ground stations. The book's dedication page reads "For a sovereign Australia", clearly still an aspiration in Ball's view. He accused the Americans of lacking candour, and Australian governments, both Labor and conservative, of shrouding signals intelligence facilities in Australia with extraordinary "secrecy, evasion and deception". He valued Pine Gap's role in arms control and verification, but also protested the particular "disdain with which the Australian people and Australia's basic interests have been treated in the establishment, maintenance and operation of the American facilities in Australia".

In 1985's *The Ties that Bind*, Ball and Jeffrey T. Richelson, an American researcher, explained the origins of the Five Eyes alliance, which emerged from British–US practices during World War II and expanded in 1947 to include Canada, Australia and New Zealand as "UKUSA-collaborating Commonwealth countries". These conveniently located dominions of the British Empire are also known as Second Parties, or "islands with aerials", as one US intelligence chief called them within earshot of Stephen Lander, a former director-general of Britain's MI5.

As Ball and Richelson showed, this extensive "transnational intelligence community" is not founded on a single agreement made back in 1947, but on a set of relationships in which each party commits to gathering and analysing signals intelligence in their designated geographic zone. Between them, these countries have coordinated the building and sharing of technology, trafficking in ever-growing quantities of information gathered from telegrams, calls and data through satellite and fibre-optic cables. By the end of the Cold War, the Five Eyes had agreements with an outer tier of countries known as the Fourteen Eyes, and a further group encompassing thirty-six countries, spanning the globe to gather intelligence through the ECHELON system, which intercepts private and commercial communications, and other systems that gather fax, radio, telephone and internet signals.

It is difficult to identify all of the offices, training grounds and facilities owned, used, leased and occupied to support the US–Australia alliance and the Five Eyes in Australia, as many are concealed or have multiple functions. While US and Australian personnel exchanges, defence trade cooperation and joint exercises are conducted openly, information collection and exchange between Five Eyes partners is far more opaque. Some intelligence gathered at Australian bases is for US and Australian use, while other material is shared among the Five Eyes partners or the wider intelligence networks.

The box on page 44 gives a brief description of the major US–Australian intelligence facilities in Australia. These include the Shoal Bay Receiving Station outside of Darwin, the Kojarena defence satellite communication facility near Geraldton, the North West Cape naval communications station above Exmouth and the Pine Gap satellite surveillance base near Alice Springs.

A senior research associate at the US-based Nautilus Institute for Security and Instability, Australian researcher Richard Tanter, asserts that "Pine Gap is perhaps the most important United States intelligence facility outside that country". He notes that it plays a vital role in the collection of a very wide range of signals intelligence, providing early warning of ballistic missile launches, targetting of nuclear weapons, providing battlefield intelligence data for United States armed forces operating in Afghanistan and elsewhere (including previously in Iraq), critically supporting United States and Japanese missile defence, supporting arms control verification, and contributing targetting data to United States drone attacks.

In September 2006, when shadow defence minister and Opposition leader Kim Beazley met with US ambassador Robert McCallum, he described Pine Gap as one of the "core elements"

Electronic surveillance capacity at the Five Eyes sites has doubled since 2000

of the US–Australia defence alliance, along with visits from warships and joint exercises. We know this thanks to diplomatic cables published in 2010 by WikiLeaks.

Since the US and Australian governments signed the Pine Gap treaty on 9 December 1966 and the facility became operational on 19 June 1970, its desert landscape has sprouted thirty-three antennas, nineteen covered by radomes – white domes designed to protect from weather and to obscure the direction an antenna faces and so which satellite it is trained on. The base's role and capabilities continue to expand. From Snowden's leaks, we learned of "Torus", an advanced quasi-parabolic multi-beam antenna that can pick up signals from thirty-five satellites concurrently due to its shape. One such antenna was installed at Pine Gap in 2008.

These new insights led Ball and others to estimate in 2015 that the electronic surveillance capacity at the Five Eyes sites has doubled since 2000. The Torus antenna alone is believed to have trebled Pine Gap's coverage of global commercial satellites. Ball described a fundamental transformation of Pine Gap, from its initial "highly specialised mission" to a "multi-agency, multi-purpose mega-intelligence centre". For decades, Ball had asserted that Pine Gap was legitimate and necessary due to its role in arms control, though he was critical of the disdain with which the United States treated Australia over joint facilities. But in 2014 he withdrew his qualified support for the base, stating that it had become "ethically unacceptable" due to its role in drone strikes.

The first Snowden documents focusing on Australia became available in August 2017 through a joint investigation by the ABC's Peter Cronau and *The Intercept*'s Ryan Gallagher. All dealt with Pine Gap, providing detailed insight into the intelligence relationship between the Australian government and the NSA as at April 2013. We learned that through the bases at Pine Gap, Shoal Bay and Kojarena, Australia is solely responsible for interception of signals intelligence on "multiple targets in the Pacific area, including Indonesia, Malaysia and Singapore", and that it contributes to US surveillance efforts regarding China and to military operations in Afghanistan. In the final section of one document, headed "Problems or Challenges with the Partner", the NSA lists "none". We also learned that the chief of the facility is accountable to the director of the US National Reconnaissance Office, and the deputy chief is a senior Australian Signals Directorate official.

A document dated 23 August 2012 highlighted the extent to which Australia is aware of Pine Gap's functions:

> RAINFALL [Pine Gap] will not be operated for any purpose without the Full Knowledge and Compliance (FK&C) of the Government of Australia (GOA) ... The GOA has the right of access to the full product of the facility through procedures established in NSA/CSS-DSD agreements and practices. The U.S. and Australia agreed to the principles of FK&C in the 1976 Implementing Arrangement for JDFPG [Joint Defense Facility Pine Gap]. FK&C is important so that the Australian Government can assure the Australian Parliament and the Australian people that all activities conducted at JDFPG are managed with the GOA's full agreement and understanding.

In 1988, the phrase "full knowledge and concurrence" was introduced by the Hawke government to counter years of public concern – and apprehension within the Australian Labor Party – that the bases represented a loss of sovereignty. The Snowden cache also included a security classification guide for the information that could be divulged about Pine Gap. This revealed the existence of a signals intelligence mission at the base, and that it provides support to NATO operations, all of which are classified "secret". The intelligence mission was supposed to be kept confidential for twenty-five years from 2009.

A document dated 24 May 2005 provides the cover story for Pine Gap, stating:

> The Joint Defense Facility Pine Gap (JDFPG) is a joint US/ Australian defense facility whose function is to support the national security of both the US and Australia. The JDFPG contributes to verifying arms control and disarmament agreements and monitoring of military developments. The JDFPG is jointly staffed by US and Australian DoD [Department of Defence] civilians and members of the various military branches.

This text is almost word for word what Prime Minister Hawke told the Australian parliament on 22 November 1988: "Pine Gap is a satellite ground station whose function is to collect intelligence data which supports the national security of both Australia and the US ... intelligence collected at Pine Gap contributes importantly to the verification of arms control and verification agreements."

Nearly all official Australian government statements have stuck to this line ever since.

A right to know

In 1980, Ball asserted a general principle: that the Australian public should know as much about US operations in Australia as does Soviet intelligence. But how could the Australian public be given access to information not even known to prime ministers? John Gorton, prime minister from 1968 to 1971, stated to journalist David Marr in 1978, "I don't even know what Pine Gap is all about. I didn't then. I could have asked but it didn't arise." William McMahon, prime minister from 1971 to 1972, said in 1977 that while he believed he knew the true functions of Pine Gap while he was in office, since then he had had "increasing doubts that the Australian government knows the entire

[The committee] was perhaps designed to overlook more than oversee

truth". Gough Whitlam told parliament in May 1977 his government did not know that information obtained at US facilities was made available to private American companies, that the first US officer-in-charge of the base was from the CIA, or that Pine Gap was a CIA operation.

Australia's public knew little more about its intelligence agencies. The Australian Signals Directorate (ASD) – which until 2013 was known as the Defence Signals Directorate, or DSD – was established in 1947 and not publicly acknowledged until 1977, existing in the shadows of the budget and policy machinery for a full three decades.

The Australian Secret Intelligence Service (ASIS) was established in 1952, publicly acknowledged in 1977 and not given a legislative basis until 2001. The existence of the ten Australian intelligence organisations that participate in Five Eyes is no longer shrouded in secrecy; indeed, they all have websites. The ASD has the main Five Eyes signals intelligence responsibilities, with the Defence Intelligence Organisation (DIO), Australian Secret Intelligence Service (ASIO) and the Australian Federal Police in supportive roles.

Parliamentary oversight in Australia is notionally provided by the Parliamentary Joint Committee on Intelligence and Security. It has a limited membership of eleven, with six drawn from the House of Representatives and five from the Senate. Currently it is chaired by Andrew Hastie, a Liberal MP, and includes six Liberal and five Labor MPs, with no crossbench representatives. (Andrew Wilkie, who sat on the committee from 2010 to 2013, was the only crossbencher ever to be among its ranks.) Much of its business is conducted in closed meetings, as it reviews the finances of intelligence organisations, updates a list of terrorist groups and examines reference requests from government. It cannot initiate reviews or examine "the intelligence-gathering and assessment priorities" or "sources of information" – it is limited to considering administrative and expenditure matters. It was perhaps designed to overlook more than to oversee.

While CIA and NSA documents can be requested under US freedom of information legislation, none of the documents produced by

Australia's intelligence organisations, or by any Cabinet-level security memos or papers, is subject to freedom of information. There are significant legal barriers to accessing information from current and former staff of intelligence agencies or publishing their identities. The *National Security Legislation Amendment Act (No. 1) 2014* imposes jail sentences of up to five years for anyone disclosing information about a "special intelligence operation", even if that person does not realise the information relates to an operation. Such are the barriers for researchers and citizens seeking to know and contribute to the discussion about what Australia actually does as part of the US–Australia defence alliance and the Five Eyes network.

How US bases limit Australia's options

In September 2016, to mark the fiftieth anniversary of the signing of the Pine Gap treaty, several hundred people travelled to Australia's red centre to protest the base's operations and the confidentiality surrounding these. They followed thousands who have made similar journeys since 1970 to camp along the fence line that separates public from secret space, or Australian from American territory. Every few years people take the trouble to congregate at the site, to remind the public of its existence and to express alarm at what is happening there, despite the cost of getting to the remote location. They understand the low likelihood of halting the activities conducted within the base's perimeters, the high risk of arousing ongoing surveillance, and the occasional hostility of locals who perceive Alice Springs as economically dependent on the base. Interviews I undertook for my PhD with twenty-seven participants revealed the main motivation at the 2016 protest was concern about Pine Gap's role in implicating Australia in US wars. Other reasons, listed in order of importance to participants, were: a desire to build a stronger peace movement; concern about drones; unease over nuclear dangers; worry about the state of Australia's democracy and its independence; wariness regarding surveillance activities; and a desire to show solidarity with local Aboriginal people over the use to which their traditional land has been put.

These protesters' views are not widely shared by Australians. According to the 2018 Lowy Institute Poll, trust in the United States fell after Donald Trump's election to its lowest recorded level. Nonetheless, this didn't prevent support for the US–Australia alliance itself, with 76 per cent saying the alliance is either very or fairly important for Australia's security. While 56 per cent of Australians believe that the alliance makes us safer from attack, 69 per cent also feel that the alliance makes it more likely we will be drawn into wars not in our interest. This is hardly surprising, given Australia's tendency to dutifully participate in US wars, and the now permanent stationing of US marines in the Northern Territory under an agreement negotiated by Julia Gillard and Barack Obama as part of America's "Pivot to Asia".

During the 2016 Pine Gap protests, six people were arrested for entering the base, all motivated by their religious faith. The government devoted significant resources to prosecuting the group – five Christians and one pagan – in two jury trials, including consulting with the US government on whether to pursue criminal charges, and flying police witnesses from around the country to give testimony. Two Director of Public Prosecutions officials advised on proceedings, and a solicitor was sent by the attorney-general's office and the Department of Defence to prevent the viewing of CCTV footage. The QCs representing the government sought years in jail for the protesters. Due to lack of funds, the protesters represented themselves, paying instead in time, stress and travel. While the protesters admitted to – and were found guilty of – entering the base, small fines of several hundred to several thousand dollars were imposed, payment for which has yet to be sought.

Fraser concluded that Pine Gap is the main barrier to a more-independent foreign policy

A turning point during the two-week trial occurred when the judge allowed a seven-minute ABC Radio interview with former prime minister Malcolm Fraser to be played to the jury. All in the court heard his distinctive voice echoing the concerns shared by the defendants about the role of Pine Gap in nuclear and conventional wars and drone strikes, and in the undermining of Australia's potential for an independent foreign policy.

US–Australia Intelligence and Surveillance Facilities

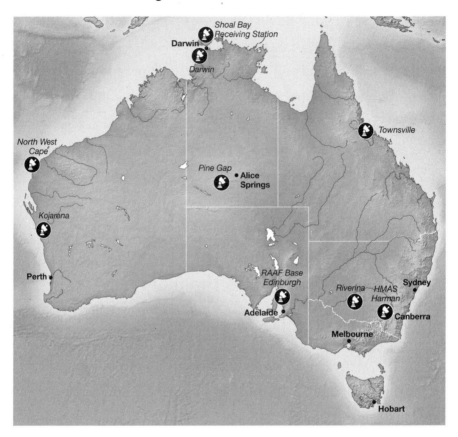

Shoal Bay Receiving Station
Location: east of Darwin, Northern Territory
Functions: intercepts satellite communications and high-frequency signals; was used to penetrate the Indonesian telephone system in the Australia–Indonesia spying scandal that made headlines in 2013
In operation: since 1979

Kojarena
Location: east of Geraldton, Western Australia
Functions: intercepts satellite and phone communications over the Indian Ocean and within South-East Asia; assists in US keyword monitoring
In operation: since 1993 (operations expanded after 2008)

North West Cape
Location: north of Exmouth, Western Australia
Functions: runs remote-operated space surveillance telescope and radar, feeds data to US space operations center; the communications station supports nuclear armed submarines and offensive nuclear weapons
In operation: since 1974 (operations extended for twenty-five years from 2008)

Pine Gap
Location: west of Alice Springs, Northern Territory
Functions: collects signals intelligence, provides early warning of ballistic missile launches, delivers targeting for nuclear weapons and drone assassinations, provides battlefield data for US military, verifies arms control
In operation: since 1970

RAAF Base Edinburgh
Location: north of Adelaide, South Australia
Functions: generates intelligence satellite data; operates radar, cooperating with Lockheed Martin for possible integration of Pine Gap data; runs remote-operated radar and telescope in collaboration with the United States; houses a surveillance drone home base
In operation: since 1955

HMAS Harman
Location: Canberra, Australian Capital Territory
Function: processing communications and intelligence data, including data from Pine Gap
In operation: since 1943

High-Frequency Direction Finding Stations
Location: Darwin, Townsville, North West Cape, Riverina
Functions: nodes on (distributes information from) the US National Security Agency's worldwide geolocation service
In operation: stations, since before World War II; the new Modernised High-Frequency Communications System (MHFCS), which coordinates with the NSA network, became operational in stages in the late 2000s

The author is grateful to Richard Tanter for his assistance in compiling this information.

Fraser's reversal of opinion on Pine Gap carried weight because of his roles as defence minister and prime minister, as well as his attempt during the Whitlam dismissal to amplify the controversy over the lease renewal on Pine Gap, which had recently been revealed to have significant CIA connections. In 1977, Fraser, as prime minister, extended the Pine Gap treaty for a further ten years, underlining its importance for Australia's relationship with the United States. In his 2014 book, *Dangerous Allies*, he defended this position, arguing that Australia's strategic dependence on the United Kingdom and then the United States was initially justifiable, but became dangerous after the end of the Cold War. He believed Pine Gap, through its expanding role, exposed Australians to prosecution for war crimes or crimes against humanity because it was used to conduct extrajudicial drone attacks on countries with which we were not at war:

> In the beginning, Pine Gap was defensive in character. The new uses to which the information it gathers can be put transforms Pine Gap into a critical part of an offensive weapons system. Australia should not be a part of it ... We cannot deny the facility's existence; neither could we dictate to the Americans that the information it gathers must not be used for the targeting of their weapons. We can hardly say to our neighbours that we are not complicit in American drone killings when the real-time information our facility collects is used for that purpose.

Fraser concluded that Pine Gap is the main barrier to Australia forming a more-independent foreign policy or establishing "some elements of strategic independence within the alliance". He assumed that "Australians would be more concerned if they realised the way in which this nominally defence system interacts with the deadly logic of deterrence in a world with thousands of nuclear weapons". But he could hardly have been surprised Australians do not realise this, given his own complicity in refusing to confirm whether Pine Gap was a nuclear target during his prime ministership – as it was, and remains. He continued the tradition of keeping Australians in the dark, which commenced when Pine Gap was established in 1967 and Minister for Defence Sir Allen Fairhall stated it would not do "anything of military significance". This was always untrue: military operations depend on intelligence, and cannot succeed without it.

In a recent evaluation of the future of the US–Australia alliance, academic Hugh White addresses fears and anxieties arising from the United States' declining power, identifying questions rarely acknowledged due to our faith in Washington's enduring protection and to assumptions that there is no alternative. His ambitious book *How to Defend Australia* grapples with the capability, force structure and purchasing decisions faced by policymakers should the ANZUS Treaty live up to its non-binding nature and China come to dominate our region. White admits Australia's own surveillance depends heavily on American systems, but barely explores the vast investment needed to build an independent intelligence capacity.

According to White, "America has remained our ally for so long because the alliance has cost it very little, and it has helped support America's leadership in Asia". He suggests that the alliance may weaken as America steps back from regional leadership, "and quite possibly disappear, as our alliance with Britain weakened and disappeared". But this doesn't account for the United States' reliance on strategic facilities in Australia for its own defence, which have involved substantial costs to establish a large signals intelligence infrastructure. Nor does it seem to recognise that Australian, US and British military surveillance and command-and-control structures have become thoroughly enmeshed through seventy years of building interoperable and interdependent systems at places such as North West Cape, Kojarena and Pine Gap. Installations that play key functions in global systems cannot be easily replaced, particularly because of their location. While the rent on North West Cape is one peppercorn per year, its location for submarine communications is priceless.

White also fails to acknowledge the risk to Australia from nuclear weapons that facilities such as Pine Gap present. "Is there really any possibility that China, India or anyone else would launch a nuclear attack on Australia? The answer is almost certainly no," he writes. Ball argued that Pine Gap's role in facilitating nuclear warfighting meant that it was a likely nuclear target during the Cold War, given that the Soviet Union gave highest priority to striking early-warning and associated command-and-control systems. There is little reason for Russia to have changed its posture, and every reason for China to have adopted it. While US planners acknowledge this, Ball pointed out that Australian officials "are prone to dismiss this possibility". Prime Minister Bob Hawke broke with this tradition in his 6 June 1984 statement, admitting that "hosting the facilities does bring with it some degree of added risk of nuclear attack". This statement was followed by Foreign Minister Bill Hayden, who, a month later, said "it is undeniable that in certain circumstances these facilities [Pine Gap, Nurrungar and North West Cape] could be nuclear targets". Beazley told the Joint Standing Committee on Foreign Affairs, Defence and Trade in 1997 that "we accepted that the joint facilities were probably targets, but we accepted the risk of that for what we saw as the benefits of global stability".

Anxieties about Australia's security future persist in policy and academic circles

White's book addresses a potential shift in global stability as China rises. But much of the Cold War doctrine, posture and targeting will be retained if Australia merely replaces the Soviet/Russian threat with geopolitical rivalry with China. And White's approach, along with much analysis of the changing power balance in Asia, fails to acknowledge the extent to which Australia's defence and foreign policy options are limited by its involvement in US intelligence and military activities.

An alliance in flux

As we approach our second century of "mateship" with the United States, Australian policy statements assert that the US–Australia alliance is central to our future, that the security guarantee is firm, that extended deterrence averts nuclear perils and that the surveillance facilities on our shores offer us information superiority. But anxieties about Australia's security future persist in policy and academic circles, including among former prime ministers and foreign ministers. Australia's current foreign minister, Marise Payne, acknowledged our need to look after ourselves during the August 2019 visit by US secretary of state Mike Pompeo (albeit issuing her statement using US spelling): "We do have to recognize that we are in an era of strategic competition and we must play our part in protecting our interests." Such an approach should involve a more open and honest discussion about the role of Pine Gap and other bases, including whether Canberra should exercise greater control over these facilities to ensure they are serving Australian interests.

Australia has increasingly affirmed support for a rules-based order as a way to bolster regional and domestic security. But this entails that Australia should join only legal and United Nations–sanctioned military action with its allies. We apparently enjoy "full knowledge and concurrence" of what occurs at US-linked bases on our soil, yet, as Malcolm Fraser suggested, knowledge and concurrence of the United States' drone program would expose Australian personnel to international legal instruments such as the

International Criminal Court statute, and to the possibility of violent retribution.

The ostensible purpose of Pine Gap was to promote nuclear non-proliferation. This is a laudable goal, yet the US bases in Australia are an impediment to achieving it. The Treaty on the Prohibition of Nuclear Weapons, outlawing the development, testing, production, stockpiling, stationing, transfer, use and threat of use of nuclear weapons, currently has eighty signatories and thirty-four ratifications. It arose from an Australian initiative that won the Nobel Peace Prize, and now is close to entering force. Australia will only be able to comply with the treaty if the United States shuts down the relay ground station at Pine Gap that supports nuclear warfighting systems. Alternatively, Australia could seek assurances to prevent this ground station and other systems from being used for nuclear planning, leaving the rest of the facility focused on signals intelligence.

But there are also questions about Australia's role in signals intelligence sharing, particularly after Snowden revealed the extent to which surveillance technologies are integrated with the internet. Snowden explained – initially to three aghast journalists in a Hong Kong hotel room, and through them to the world – the way that US intelligence agencies place back doors in software and hardware, rendering much online infrastructure vulnerable, from mobile-phone devices to server stacks to email clients to payment mechanisms. Browsers are infected. Encryption standards have been deliberately weakened. Submarine fibre-optic cables have been tapped. Even offline devices can be "illuminated" and their data read. According to Snowden, the entire internet is owned by the NSA and its Five Eyes partners, including all the networked phone and computer devices in the hands of individuals, heads of state and their spouses.

In response, academics Patrick Walsh and Seumas Miller assert that Five Eyes procedures and policies should be based on ethical guidelines to improve intelligence collection while managing the risks to human rights and data security. To propose that indiscriminate intelligence collection can corrode democracy is not to deny that surveillance powers in the hands of law enforcement, national security and surveillance agencies have a legitimate role. Measures such as judicial warrants and ministerial and parliamentary oversight have been designed to grant those agencies lawfulness, legitimacy and social licence as much as to prevent overreach. But violating the privacy of citizens or the sovereignty, dignity and privacy of other states can do more to threaten than to protect the people and the nation.

Accurate and honest information about the capabilities, costs and benefits of facilities such as Pine Gap is virtually non-existent, and what is known has only trickled through after overcoming official resistance. This is why these facilities rarely enter public debate on Australia's defences or its approach to Asia or the world. Yet it is crucial for Australia to make informed choices within a region of fluctuating tensions about the costs and benefits of being embroiled in current and future US military operations and plans for nuclear war. ■

MESSAGE TO WASHINGTON

How to maximise
US strength in Asia

Brendan Taylor

Canberra today has one major foreign policy dilemma that outranks all others: how should Australia position itself between a more powerful China and an increasingly unpredictable United States?

The debate it provokes has become a dialogue of the deaf, in which entrenched positions prevent the two sides from arriving at a solution. Understandably, yet unhelpfully, the weighty moral and material issues at play give the discussion an increasingly nasty, personalised edge. As Allan Gyngell, national president of the Australian Institute of International Affairs, has noted, "The debate is getting sharper. Commentators and analysts from the think tanks and universities are marshalling themselves into hostile camps."

In one corner are the China hawks, who contend that Canberra should stand up to Beijing, alongside Washington, preserving the US-led order in Asia that has served Australia so well. This entails bringing India into the fold, through such mechanisms as the Indo-Pacific framework and the Quadrilateral Security Dialogue, to balance an increasingly boisterous China and force it to play by international rules.

In the opposing corner are those who argue that US power is in precipitous decline and that America's longstanding presence in Asia can no longer be counted on. According to this view, a weakened United States will ultimately play little, if any, role in this region. Australia must find new ways of living in a world dominated by China. It may even need to learn to fend for itself militarily.

Both sides are wrong. The United States, whose military strength and spending remain unmatched, shows little inclination for abandoning Asia. Despite President Trump's "America First" utterances, competition with China has become his administration's primary national security concern. US attitudes towards Beijing are hardening across partisan lines and even among the traditionally pro-China business community. A growing number of commentators now speak of a new Sino–American Cold War. But it is equally unrealistic to expect Asia's existing security order to remain intact as seismic shifts continue in this region's power dynamics and as China's strength and assertiveness grows.

A third way is needed, one that acknowledges both America's power in Asia and its limitations. And there is no need to invent this approach because it already exists – there is a plan, devised by eminent Cold War strategist and diplomat Dean Acheson, that applies to the contemporary moment, in which America faces the most serious challenge yet to its decades-long global dominance.

At the start of the Cold War, in the early 1950s, Washington confronted an aggressive, expansionist Moscow bent on world domination. Where and how to best counter the Soviet threat was a source of fierce debate. Acheson's response was to call for the United States to create "situations of strength": areas around the Soviet periphery where America was so strong that Moscow wouldn't even contemplate aggression there. George F. Kennan, another leading architect of US Cold War strategy, favoured a minimalist approach. If "strong points" of defence could be established in Japan – which Kennan saw as one of the few centres of power with the industrial, population and military potential to challenge America – he believed that any Soviet threat to the United States in Asia could be readily contained. Others, such as strategist Paul Nitze, took a much darker view of Soviet intentions, and argued that threats to freedom anywhere were a challenge to US security that had to be quashed.

The United States' strategy in Asia is dangerously directionless

Acheson's approach prevailed, though its implementation was at times muddled. He was castigated for dismissing the need for a US situation of strength in Korea. His neglect invited North Korea's invasion of the South, resulting in the cruel and bitter Korean War of the early 1950s. In other places the United States overstretched, most infamously in Vietnam, when it devoted substantial military assets to a country of questionable strategic relevance in the larger contest against the Soviet Union. But even as America's Cold War tactics changed, Acheson's situations of strength remained a strategic lodestar.

In contrast, the United States' strategy in Asia is now dangerously directionless. Much like Trump's scrawling, oversized signature, this administration paints in broad and imprecise brushstrokes. A core aim, according to the US Department of Defense's June 2019 Indo-Pacific Strategy Report, is ensuring a "favourable" balance of power across this vast region, which it defines as encompassing around half of the planet's surface. Trump's post–Cold War predecessors – Bushes senior and junior, Bill Clinton and Barack Obama – pursued similar grand ambitions. But they were operating in an era of uncontested US primacy. Trump's reality is different. The period that the late conservative commentator Charles Krauthammer in 1990 dubbed the "unipolar moment" has passed.

America can remain a powerful player in Asia if it quickly recognises this new power dynamic and develops a plan to preserve its interests and maximise its position in the region. To do that, Washington must identify today's situations of strength and double down on them. But it must also be more attuned to where its strength is slipping. It must begin extricating itself from emerging situations of weakness. Alas, Trump is lurching in exactly the opposite direction, leaning in on positions in Asia where the United States is at its weakest. Dean Acheson must be turning in his grave.

Situations of strength

When World War II ended, America was at the height of its power. The United States produced 60 per cent of the globe's gross national product. It held a monopoly on the atomic bomb, the most powerful weapon the world had ever seen. Due to this, Winston Churchill bristled at Acheson's theory of situations of strength, believing that America did not need to create offensive positions in a time of uncontested power.

The United States is nowhere near as predominant today. But it is still a formidable power. The 2019 Lowy Institute Asia Power Index ranks it as the region's strongest player, based on attributes such as economic relationships, military capacity, diplomatic and cultural influence, and future resources.

The nation's lead in military capacity is especially pronounced, partly due to the substantial sums it spends on defence. According to the latest figures from the International Institute for Strategic Studies, the United States is the world's biggest military spender, boasting an annual defence budget of US$643.3 billion. China spends US$168.2 billion, just over a quarter of that sum. Elsewhere in Asia, India is the world's fifth-largest (US$57.9 billion) and Japan the eighth-largest (US$47.3 billion) defence spender. Australia sits in twelfth position, with an annual defence budget of US$26.6 billion.

The United States is also the world's leading cyberpower. Strength in this rapidly evolving area is hard to quantify. Countries such as China and Russia are building their cyber capabilities at an impressive rate, potentially faster than the United States. America's heavy reliance on computer networks for warfighting also creates potential vulnerabilities. But while the United States might not remain the world's pre-eminent cyberpower indefinitely, it continues to reap the considerable "first mover" advantages, having developed a number of critical technologies, including the internet.

American strength in Asia is reinforced by its alliance relationships. Nowhere is this clearer than with Japan, which successive generations of US officials have described as the "cornerstone" of America's Asian presence. The United States bases 53,900 military personnel there, primarily US Air Force and Navy, spread across eighty-five different facilities.

Japan has its own impressive air and naval capabilities, which augment US strength. Aside from the United States, it is probably the only other power in Asia that could hold its own in a maritime conflict with China. While its force is small – Japan has only forty-nine large-surface ships and twenty submarines, compared with China's eighty-seven surface combatants and fifty-nine submarines – it makes up for this in quality. Anti-submarine warfare, for example, is a known area of Chinese weakness where Japan's capabilities are second to none.

The US and Japanese militaries work increasingly hand-in-glove in Asia. They jointly operate a string of underwater sensors that stretches from the Ryukyu Islands in southern Japan right across to Taiwan. These are used to track Chinese submarines travelling between the East and South China seas, as well as between the East China Sea and the Pacific. Senior American officials have repeatedly confirmed that Chinese military action against its Asian ally in the East China Sea would trigger the Treaty of Mutual Cooperation and Security between the United States and Japan. The knowledge that it would be no match for the combined forces of America and Japan is a powerful deterrent for China's leaders. This makes the East China Sea a clear situation of strength for the United States.

Should trends continue, the United States will lose the capability to come to Taiwan's defence

The Korean Peninsula is another situation of strength. America currently deploys 28,500 troops there, the majority of these army. Their presence is designed to symbolise the US commitment to South Korea, as a force of this size would not lead to any re-run of the Korean War victory – especially against the North's million-strong army. But South Korea's military is also potent. While half the size of its northern counterpart, its armed forces are far better trained and more technologically advanced. In fact, Pyongyang's expansion of its nuclear and missile programs, and its desire to publicise these investments, is partly due to how far North Korea's military has fallen behind its neighbour's.

South Korea's imposing armed forces would automatically come under US command in the event of conflict. While South Korean president Moon Jae-in has promised to end this longstanding arrangement by the conclusion of his presidency in 2022, for now it adds considerable strength to America's arm.

Situations of weakness

Yet US strength is slipping elsewhere in Asia. Take Taiwan: when America's alliance with the island formally lapsed at the end of 1979 – the chief casualty of US–China diplomatic normalisation – Taipei could still have held its own in a clash with the mainland. Taiwan's major surface ships outnumbered China's by forty to twenty-five, unthinkable as that seems today. Alliance with the United States also provided Taipei with access to superior technology, while more than twenty other countries were willing to sell the island weapons. But Chinese pressure has since forced them to abandon Taipei, leaving the United States as essentially Taiwan's sole arms supplier.

Angered at Washington's betrayal, Taipei's friends in the US Congress enacted the *Taiwan Relations Act*, which stipulated that America retain some security ties with the island. When in 1995 and early 1996 China conducted missile tests and military exercises aimed at intimidating Taiwanese voters on the eve of their first direct presidential election, the Clinton administration responded by deploying two aircraft-carrier battle groups. Significantly, this was the largest US naval deployment to Asia since the end of the Vietnam War.

Clinton's display of force was intended to show resolve at a time when those in the region worried that the United States might withdraw, having seen off the Soviet Union and its threat of communism. However, it also had an unintended consequence: in forcing a humiliating Chinese backdown, it motivated Beijing to develop the military wherewithal to stop the United States from coming to Taiwan's aid.

Since then, China's march toward military modernisation has progressed at an impressive rate. Two decades after the 1995–96 crisis, Beijing has largely achieved its aim. It has developed increasingly powerful anti-shipping missiles, such as the Dongfeng 21D (DF-21D) – dubbed the "carrier killer" because of its capacity to strike aircraft carriers out to a range of 1550 kilometres. At its National Day parade in October 2019, China unveiled two more missiles – the DF-41 intercontinental ballistic missile and the DF-17 short-range ballistic missile. The DF-41 can strike continental United States. Unlike its liquid-operated predecessors, which need to be fuelled at the launchpad – thus making them easier for an opponent to target – the DF-41 is solid-fuelled and road-mobile (able to be transported easily), making it much harder to take out. The DF-17 is also the world's first "hypersonic" missile, meaning it can fly at five times the speed of sound. Current missile defence systems cannot reliably track and intercept missiles travelling at this speed.

Through the development of advanced radar, sonar and satellite technologies, China has also improved its ability to aim these missiles. The DF-21D and the DF-17, for example, can now strike within metres of their assigned targets. This stands in stark contrast to the mid-1990s, when China had virtually no capacity to hit even large US military bases in Asia. It remains to be seen how these technologies would perform in the heat of battle. Modelling by the RAND Corporation suggests that the costs and risks of US intervention in a conflict over Taiwan have increased substantially over the past two decades. According to RAND, in 1996 the United States could have achieved air superiority over China within a week of entering such a conflict, using only a single air wing of seventy-two fighter aircraft; by 2017, the country would have needed three to four air wings, while the time required to achieve air superiority increased to three weeks. Should these trends continue, the United States will lose the capability to come to Taiwan's defence successfully. That tipping point could conceivably come within the next decade.

Trump either did not receive or has not read this memo. Relations between America and Taiwan are now the closest they have been since US–China normalisation. In 2016, president-elect Trump became the first head of state to speak directly with Taipei since 1979 when he took a congratulatory phone call from the island's independence-leaning leader, Tsai Ing-wen. In March 2018, he signed the *Taiwan Travel Act*, allowing US government officials at all levels to meet with their Taiwanese counterparts and so making public interactions that had previously been occurring in secret. Trump has approved multi-billion-dollar weapons sales to the island, including F-16V fighter jets (the most advanced version of that aircraft) and

Abrams tanks. US Navy ships now transit the Taiwan Strait monthly, while the Indo-Pacific Strategy Report took the unprecedented step of referring to Taiwan as a country. All this has created the worst of two worlds: it has raised Beijing's ire to boiling point, while giving Taipei false hope.

A similar pattern is developing over the South China Sea. It is important not to exaggerate China's ability to project military power across this vast 3.7-million-square-kilometre body of water. China has only two aircraft carriers – the key means of projecting military power in the area – and the first was acquired second-hand from Ukraine. A third is currently under construction and is expected to enter service by 2022.

The South China Sea is fast becoming a Chinese lake once more

Some experts believe that China envisages a fleet of four to six aircraft carriers. Even so, this is much smaller than the US carrier fleet, which currently numbers ten. The US carriers are also much larger than their Chinese counterparts, allowing them to accommodate twice as many aircraft, and they are nuclear-powered, which gives them significantly greater range than China's conventionally propelled boats.

Beijing's much-publicised construction of artificial islands in this sea can also be seen as a sign of weakness. Work on these features began in 2013, when Chinese dredgers began to "reclaim" the equivalent of 3000 football ovals of territory by digging sand from the seabed and dumping it onto disputed rocks and reefs. Reports have since emerged that these islands are starting to succumb to the South China Sea's unforgiving climate. In October 2019, *The Economist* reported that their foundations are turning to sponge. If true, it is unlikely such fragile features will survive one of the region's super-typhoons, not to mention the barrage of air and missile strikes in the event of a full-blown conflict. Size, once again, matters. If war erupted, these features would not be large enough to sustain the required numbers of troops and missiles, or even basic rations and electricity.

Nonetheless, senior US military officials – including Indo-Pacific Commander Admiral Phil Davidson – concede that these artificial features, while they exist, give Beijing control over the South China Sea in all situations short of war. Reinforcing these claims, in May 2018 China landed its most capable strategic bomber aircraft – the H-6K – at one of these outposts for the first time. The landing took place on Woody Island, part of the Paracel chain in the northern South China Sea. Aircraft hangars have been built on several features further south, in the Spratly chain. It is only a matter of time before Chinese bombers are landing and taking off from these outposts too – which are significantly closer to Australian shores.

China has also installed powerful anti-shipping and anti-aircraft missiles on bases in both the Paracels and the Spratlys. This is despite Chinese president Xi Jinping's September 2015 pledge, while standing alongside Obama in the Rose Garden of the White House, that Beijing had no intention of militarising the South China Sea.

A struggling superpower

Washington's current approach reveals weakness, not strength. President Obama upped the rate of "freedom of navigation operations" (or FONOPS) in the South China Sea, and Trump has continued this pattern. FONOPS involve military ships and aircraft travelling within 12 nautical miles of China's artificial features, thereby challenging China's attempts to restrict navigation and overflight of the waters surrounding this territory. But such shows of force have neither stopped Beijing's massive land reclamation program nor slowed its militarisation of the South China Sea. And not a single Asian country has been willing to undertake similar operations, either alone or alongside America. This includes Australia, which has been under continual pressure from the United States to step up. In a response to James Brown's 2016 Quarterly Essay *Firing Line*, former Australian ambassador to the United States Kim Beazley recalls the parting gift he received when leaving Washington: a picture of a US destroyer being tailed by a Chinese ship while conducting a South China Sea FONOP. It carried an inscription, scribbled by a senior American official: "Hope to see your guys doing this soon."

But geography favours China too strongly in these growing situations of weakness. Taiwan is 11,000 kilometres away from the continental United States. It sits less than 200 kilometres from the Chinese mainland. Although America still spends an estimated 700 "ship days" each year in the South China Sea – meaning that at least two US military vessels are sailing there at almost any given time – Beijing's ability, as a littoral state, to force America to operate further away from China's shores is only improving. The South China Sea is fast becoming a Chinese lake once more, just as it was from the fourteenth through to the early seventeenth century, when the powerful Ming dynasty ruled its waves.

Some commentators state that America can turn the tide by augmenting its presence in the South China Sea: by increasing the number of ships, aircraft and submarines it operates in these waters, by performing exercises more regularly with its Asian partners and by providing its South-East Asian allies with more-potent military equipment, including drones, mines, missiles and air-defence systems. Ely Ratner, one-time adviser to Joe Biden – formerly US vice president and now a frontrunner for the Democratic Party's presidential nomination – even goes so far as to suggest that the United States should be helping other South-East Asian claimants with their own land reclamation efforts and with fortifying the features they occupy.

But such an approach would spread the United States too thin. Washington already confronts what a key report from the University of Sydney's United States Studies Centre describes as "a deepening crisis of strategic insolvency". A decade of funding restrictions, delays and uncertainties have contributed to this quagmire. The operational and maintenance costs of the US military are already exceeding inflation. The American public has no appetite for increased defence spending. In fact, mounting deficits and rising public debt mean that less of the federal budget will be available for defence in future. All this reinforces the view that the US goal of upholding a "favourable" military balance across the entire Indo-Pacific region is simply not feasible.

New Delhi's commitment to non-alignment is an even greater constraint. Two centuries of subjugation by the West has hardwired a desire for strategic autonomy into the Indian psyche. It is true that India's young population gives it one of the most promising demographic profiles in Asia. Based on current projections, India will also become the world's second-largest economy by 2050. But converting economic weight into military power takes decades, as China's experience shows. India is not the answer to the US desire to maintain a favourable power balance across Asia.

The United States could fall victim to imperial overstretch

The same is true of South-East Asia, where non-aligned preferences remain just as deep-seated. These came into sharpest relief in October 2016, when Filipino strongman Rodrigo Duterte famously announced his country's "separation" from the United States while visiting Beijing. More recently, Singapore's infinitely savvier prime minister, Lee Hsien Loong, attracted Washington's ire by calling both China and America to account in his keynote address to the May 2019 Shangri-La Dialogue: "The bottom line is that the US and China need to work together, and with other countries too, to bring the global system up to date, and to not upend the system. To succeed in this, each must understand the other's point of view and reconcile each other's interests." Interestingly, Prime Minister Scott Morrison briefly stuck his head above the parapet, musing publicly that there were many insights in Lee's speech that Australia shared.

Trump's disdain for alliances further undermines America's position in Asia. He has essentially turned a blind eye to Kim Jong-un's testing of missiles that can't reach the US homeland, even though these still threaten Japan and South Korea. In November 2019, the Pentagon was forced to deny South Korean press reports that thousands of American troops would be withdrawn from the Korean Peninsula if Seoul refused to bear more of the financial burden for keeping them there. Rumours also circulated that the US president even privately contemplated leaving the US–Japan alliance. Trump responded angrily to these speculations, raging that Tokyo had been "taking advantage" of America.

Acheson would see the writing on the wall. He would tell Trump to double down on US situations of strength in the East China Sea and on the Korean Peninsula, concentrating America's Asian military presence there and further clarifying its alliance commitments to Seoul and Tokyo. Increasing US troop levels or building new military bases would be tricky given domestic sensitivities in both South Korea and Japan. But American ships and aircraft could still operate more frequently in their surrounding waters. Statements of US support for its north-east Asian allies should also be clearer and more consistent, especially in times of crisis.

Acheson would likely call concurrently for the United States to scale down in situations of weakness in the South China Sea and around Taiwan. A new balance in Asia would result, one that better reflected this region's power realities. It would genuinely be a balance, rather than the lopsided, unrealistic and dangerously unstable order that Washington is currently fostering.

Trump might not listen. Even a president more receptive to expert opinion would struggle with this Achesonian approach. Superpowers usually think in global terms. It is challenging to pivot between regions, as Obama discovered when he tried to "rebalance" the US focus, away from Europe and towards Asia, with little success. The thought of adjusting priorities *within* a region is anathema to a superpower.

The United States has also never much liked balance-of-power politics. Americans have long regarded Europe's embrace of this approach through the sixteenth, seventeenth, eighteenth and twentieth centuries as the cause of that continent's troubles, including two world wars. And from its earliest days as a republic, the United States has seen itself as exceptional, a "shining city on the hill" for others to emulate, not a member nation working alongside others to create and maintain global equilibrium. Acheson himself recognised this reality, framing his strategic formulations in lofty, idealistic terms to make them sufficiently palatable to his fellow Americans.

Promoting a third way

Canberra faces a conundrum. If Washington continues on its present trajectory, the risk to its position in Asia will grow. The United States could fall victim to what Yale historian Paul Kennedy terms "imperial overstretch": a fate that has befallen many of the world's major powers when they have overextended economically, militarily and geographically, creating an unsustainable burden on their domestic resources. Alternatively, the United States could find itself confronting an increasingly powerful China in a situation of weakness, which would result in either a humiliating US backdown or a costly military defeat.

Neither conflict between the United States and China nor American retreat is in Australia's interest. A war of any significant length and intensity would cause China's trade, consumption and income from investment to plummet. This would likely prompt an Australian economic recession, because China is by far our largest trading partner. Should America withdraw, no Asian power or combination thereof would be able to check China.

A China-dominated region might not necessarily be bad for Australia. Beijing could yet become a benign hegemon, just as it was for hundreds of years when it sat at the centre of Asia's ancient tributary system. But China's more recent regional heavy-handedness does not augur well. Instead, a new Asian balance of power, where America stays and doubles down on situations of strength, is Australia's best bet.

Encouraging Washington to back away from situations of weakness is a risky strategy for Canberra, especially where the South China

Sea is concerned. Beijing's military outposts have already brought Chinese firepower more than 1000 kilometres closer to Australia. Up to 65 per cent of Australian trade traverses these economically vital waters.

Some commentators will assert that medium-sized nations such as Australia are powerless to influence the United States, especially during an administration as dysfunctional as Trump's. History suggests this need not be the case. During the First Taiwan Strait Crisis – in the mid-1950s, when US power was at its peak – Australian prime minister Robert Menzies worked with his counterparts in London, Ottawa and Wellington to urge American restraint and advance

Australia's leaders must have the strength to speak truth to power

diplomatic solutions. The Indo-Pacific strategy that America now promotes was developed in Canberra: Australian diplomats employed the concept of the Indo-Pacific privately from as early as the mid-2000s, and Australia was the first government in the region to officially use this now-pervasive term, in its 2013 Defence White Paper. The Indo-Pacific concept might be flawed, but Canberra's successful promotion of it shows what is possible.

Australia needs to formulate an approach to Asia's changing power balance – one that maximises America's position, but remains clear-sighted about China's strength – and convey this to Washington.

Getting through to Trump will not be easy. Morrison seems to have established a good rapport with the president, which is a useful start. But there are other angles that Canberra can and should work, including through senior interlocutors in the US Congress and the foreign policy bureaucracy. This will involve some trial and error. There is no silver bullet when dealing with such an idiosyncratic and historically unprecedented administration. Perhaps most importantly, Canberra must also remain in close contact with its Asian friends and partners, quietly advocating this third way in other regional capitals – Jakarta, New Delhi, Singapore, Seoul and Tokyo in particular. This is the essence of effective middle-power diplomacy.

At the outset of the Cold War, America was divided into rival camps. One side insisted that the United States and the Soviet Union must cooperate, as the only alternative was nuclear catastrophe. The other maintained that Washington should call Moscow's bluff and enter into a risky showdown. Acheson's counsel enabled America to chart a viable third way between appeasement and nuclear armageddon. Seven decades on, as the United States enters a new era of competition with China, his approach has renewed resonance. America is hurtling blindly towards a deadly confrontation with Beijing, one that could have dire ramifications for its continued presence in Asia. Australia's leaders must have the strength, foresight and diplomatic acumen to speak this truth to power. And they have a clear template to take with them – one that has worked before to maximise America's strength, and could work again today. ■

BEYOND TRUMP

The view from
the United States

Kelly Magsamen

Determining the future of US engagement in the Asia-Pacific at times feels like a speculative exercise that revolves around the re-election or defeat of President Donald Trump. But America's policy in Asia will be shaped by questions that extend far beyond the outcome of the presidential election in November 2020. Many of these questions revolve around China, and the challenge it poses to the interests of the United States and its allies. The nation will need not only to recast its approach to the region but also to make substantial changes at home. How will it adjust to a world in which it is no longer the only dominant global power? And can the region change with it?

Over the last decade, US policies in the Asia-Pacific have each been branded differently – from the "Pivot to Asia" to the "Free and Open Indo-Pacific" – but all have recognised the importance of the region to the American economy as well as to the security of its citizens and allies. These policies aim to promote US interests and values, including ensuring the rule of law, enabling freedom of navigation and overflight, broadening economic opportunity and advancing the universal rights of all peoples. This list now also includes managing the relationship with China.

However, America's ability to advance its regional interests is becoming more contested. No longer does the United States solely dominate the air and sea. China's massive military modernisation, combined with its assertive territorial and maritime strategy, is challenging the primacy and attendant reliability of the United States. For example, China has steadily advanced its position in the South China Sea while avoiding direct conflict, thereby undermining regional perceptions of American effectiveness and generating friction in US alliances. While the United States will likely be the key military power in the region for years to come due to the overwhelming lead it has in defence spending, its capacity to advance its foreign policy objectives purely through military dominance is increasingly in doubt.

Meanwhile, China's historic growth over the last two decades has made it the primary economic force in the region. The balance of regional trade vastly favours China – now the largest trading partner of the Association of Southeast Asian Nations (ASEAN) and of key US allies including Australia. The United States – hobbled by its withdrawal from the Trans-Pacific Partnership and its lack of a substitute regional economic vision – has retreated at the precise moment China is surging. Washington's poorly executed and self-wounding trade war with Beijing, coupled with trade spats with the European Union and key allies such as South Korea, has divided the United States from the very partners it needs to marshal collective economic pressure on China. The result is that US statecraft in the region (and globally) lacks coherence and will ultimately prove ineffective in competing with its chief economic competitor.

At the same time, these security and economic dynamics – the traditional measurements of state power – are being superseded. In this century, the most contested and important domain will be the digital and information arena, where the United States and its democratic allies are already locked in an intense competition with China. The question over

We are at a critical point for US policy in the Asia-Pacific

which country will dominate 5G technology is likely to be just the first battle in a much longer technology war that will have implications for the global economy, governance, access to information and even military conflict. So far the United States has largely chosen to fight this battle unilaterally, while attempting to line up its friends and allies almost after the fact – Australia being a major exception.

Clearly, we are at a critical point for US policy in the Asia-Pacific. The post–World War II liberal international order is no longer tenable or sufficient to meet the challenges of this century. The order has already been under stress for years, as revisionist powers such as Russia and China have eroded long-accepted rules and norms and promoted an alternative, less liberal vision. Its deterioration is being accelerated by American drift and subsequent questions around US reliability – the result both of Trump and of increasing domestic political dysfunction.

America's policymakers need to decide on the goals of its policy in the Asia-Pacific and whether it (and its allies) are well positioned to achieve them. The strategy of ensuring US dominance in all domains is outdated, and expensive to pursue; there is also little appetite for it among the American public, which is seeking a more restrained and balanced foreign policy. But it would be strategically unwise for the United States to abandon its efforts in Asia, given the scope of its long-term interests and its deep people-to-people ties. A more realistic approach than chasing primacy or pulling back would be for the United States to aim to ensure that all countries in the region can make their own security and economic choices, free from coercion.

This will require a shift in Washington's mindset. It will also require sustained and reliable US diplomatic, economic and security engagement and, in some cases, will cause intense competition with China. It will involve more collective and mutually beneficial partnerships with US friends and allies. But chiefly, it will entail the United States being able to present a credible, sustainable alternative to what the Chinese Communist Party (CCP) is offering the region and the world.

A plan for Asia begins at home

It may seem counterintuitive, but the strength of American engagement in the Asia-Pacific will depend primarily on decisions about its domestic affairs.

Recent polling by the Center for American Progress showed that the American public lacked even a basic understanding of the goals of US foreign policy. But it also showed that Americans do not want to retreat from a position of global leadership. Instead, there is a strong consensus around making decisions and investments at home that will enable us to lead abroad.

In order for its political and economic model to compete in a contested world, the United States should invest more in its greatest competitive strength: the American people. In competing with China, this will matter as much as – if not more than – what we do in the South China Sea.

Many in the region may fear that a renewed US focus on domestic policy will lead to isolationism and retrenchment. But it is the only way we will be able to sustain US strength. The basic economic and social compact with the American middle class that propelled the United States into the role of global superpower and ensured this position for decades is increasingly at risk. It is time for a new generation of leaders to make the case for the United States' role not only as a global leader but as a model of the liberal-democratic way of life.

What would investment at home look like? The United States must spend significantly more on research and development in areas such as biotechnology, on public education, on the development of the green economy and on national infrastructure. These aspects are necessary for the country to continue to shape the global economy and provide a credible alternative to China.

And it does not stop at investment. The United States needs to demonstrate to its citizens (and to the world) that it can deliver for its people and solve its most pressing domestic problems. The nation has serious governance challenges: from gun violence to poorly regulated political donations to an increasing lack of fiscal discipline. The political divide between Democrat and Republican is becoming ever wider – and it is unclear how this can be overcome without major political reforms and a new narrative of a unified America.

The United States also needs to make sound choices on where, when and how it chooses to apply its power. After almost two decades of overreliance on the military – from the global War on Terror to the South China Sea – it is time for a major reconsideration of the role that military force plays in US foreign policy. More emphasis needs to be placed on diplomatic, economic, commercial and intelligence tools – and budgets need to better reflect that balance. As of 2017, the United States put 57 per cent of its discretionary spending towards defence. The Department of State, the Department of Commerce and the United States Agency for International Development together accounted for less than 5 per cent of the federal budget. For the first time, there are now more Chinese than American diplomatic posts abroad. And, while important, the US *Better Utilization of Investment*

Leading to Development Act – which envisions about US$60 billion in development financing – is a far cry from China's Belt and Road Initiative. To be truly competitive, the United States needs an extensive and disciplined commercial strategy abroad aligned with its diplomatic objectives – something currently lacking under President Trump and Secretary of Commerce Wilbur Ross. This would entail far more coordination between the government and the private sector.

Meanwhile, US strategy and resources remain focused on counterterrorism despite erratic efforts across two administrations to address more urgent global challenges, such as China. This is due in part to bureaucratic inertia and a failure to make the necessary investments of time and resources, but also

The grand bargain of the past few decades is no longer working

to the absence of a compelling case for a foreign policy that the public can rally behind. For much of the twentieth and early twenty-first century, Americans understood in a visceral way the need to counter the threat from fascism, then communism, then terrorism. The current global context is far more complex and harder to reduce to a simple "ism". And because the United States and the world are deeply integrated economically with China, it is harder to frame the threat China poses as existential, even if it could end up being so. Although there is a growing consensus in Washington that China will be the main rival of this century, there is not yet the same consensus among the American public.

The good news is that the United States and its people have a unique and demonstrated ability to self-correct. The CCP likes to highlight US political dysfunction to emphasise the relative strengths of its system. But America has seen challenging times before: the Civil War, the Great Depression, the domestic strife over the Vietnam War and the civil rights movement, the 2008 financial crisis and, most recently, the Trump effect. The course correction America needs today requires leadership underpinned by a broader public consensus. That consensus does not yet exist – but US competition with China can, if framed correctly, be channelled to provide the rationale and impetus for change.

When to cooperate with China – and when to compete

Even in this era of heightened competition, the United States and China have a mutual interest in stabilising the world's most significant bilateral relationship. This will mean new understandings on everything from the boundaries of economic competition – how far both countries are prepared to decouple – to how to address climate change. It will also involve more meaningful and straightforward dialogue between the two nations, as well as improved channels of communication over risk management and in times of crisis.

The key to stabilisation in an era of competition will be finding ways to prevent the relationship from disintegrating into full-fledged hostility, undermining the long-term interests of the United States and its democratic allies. As Kurt M. Campbell and Jake Sullivan argued in a piece for US periodical *Foreign Affairs*, the competition must have a clear end point, rather than involve an instinctive journey without a destination.

So, what does "successfully managed" US–China competition look like, and what is the goal? Can both nations advance their interests through competition while avoiding conflict, or is it a zero-sum game?

Many academics have spoken of the Thucydides Trap – the idea that competition between a dominant and a rising power often leads to conflict – and the need for the United States and China to avoid it. But today's world is far more complex than ancient Greece prior to the Peloponnesian War. This is not even the same world that generated the Cold War rivalry between the United States and the Soviet Union. Instead, the globe's two largest economic and military powers are as co-dependent as they are rivalrous.

Not all competition is inherently negative, just as not all cooperation is innately positive. In fact, focused competition in some domains could actually prevent conflict down the line. For instance, a vigorous and organised international response, led by the United States, to China's recent efforts to impose its restrictions on freedom of speech abroad is essential to setting an early, firm boundary and to avoiding misunderstandings that could fuel broader hostility. Likewise, democracies' collective efforts to invest in global digital infrastructure today could help ensure a more free and open information domain in the years ahead. Campbell and Sullivan argue, perceptively, for "a steady state of clear-eyed coexistence on terms favorable to U.S. interests and values". The question is what level of friction it will take to get there.

The economic competition is complex, and will be difficult to resolve. In many ways, this was inevitable. The mutual grand bargain of the past few decades – a vast global market for American goods and services alongside low-cost Chinese labour – is no longer working for either country. China's unfair trade and economic practices (which are closely tethered to its domestic political stability) prevent an equal playing field, and ultimately limit its ability to escape its own economic straitjacket. China's market is increasingly less hospitable to global business, and its technology transfer policies are generating major market distortions. Can the United States and China reach an equilibrium where competition does not become counterproductive or drag on global growth?

Complete decoupling is fraught with danger for both countries and for the international community – it would remove the brakes on a broader conflict. Frankly, it may also be unrealistic. Despite Beijing's and Washington's hyper-charged claims that they do not need each other for sustained growth, the truth is more complex. China and the United States need to maintain just enough integration to raise the stakes on conflict while walling off sectors they deem critical to either their security or their economic competitiveness. So far, no one has been able to define what that looks like, allowing maximalist approaches on both sides to gain traction, but there are measures we could consider. For example, a compromise could be found in which high technology critical to national security is protected, while capital markets and mutual investment, which provide benefits to both nations, remain open.

As for national security, it is in the interests of both sides to avoid military conflict – for now. China keeps friction below the level of conflict, applying grey zone tactics – such as building artificial islands in the South China Sea – to slowly advance its strategic objectives. Meanwhile, the United States relies on traditional deterrence efforts

Trump has sown a mistrust of America's democracy

such as naval and air presence operations or regional missile defence, which have been successful at preventing an all-out war it neither wants nor can afford but have not stopped China from achieving its goals. Yet as China's military power grows, it is likely to lower its threshold for friction not just with the United States but also against its allies and partners, pushing the boundaries of coercion through force. A stronger Chinese military without an effective American or regional counterbalance would prove disastrous for the region. The conundrum for US policymakers is how to deter and (if necessary) defeat China without generating a counterproductive Chinese response or backlash in the region. And what does deterrence in a scenario of increasing military parity look like? A clear set of understandings between the United States and China will help to reduce the risk of conflict. But to deal with the Chinese military threat effectively, the United States needs an alliance strategy – a regional plan in which its allies work as much with each other as with us.

Towards a golden era of US alliances

One of America's greatest strategic assets has long been its global alliance system. Donald Trump is, unfortunately, currently stress-testing that system. But this recent attention should not disguise the fact that US alliances are based on an outmoded twentieth-century construct. US allies in the region are clearly far more capable and powerful than they were following World War II, and they face a much more complex operating environment. Yet US alliances too often remain caught up in the sweeping rhetoric of history – which awkwardly patches over the fissures, such as the 2003 Iraq War or the latest confusion over US Middle East policy. As a result, it is very easy for US (and regional) policymakers to treat these alliances as a fixed common good. But the United States and its allies need to reconsider what purpose these alliances serve in the twenty-first century. Are they purely defence and security arrangements? Are the understandings and values that underpin them clear and relevant? What are the mutual expectations, and do these need to be adjusted in a changing Asia?

To grapple with these questions, it is necessary to confront the issue of American reliability. Many in the region are now questioning the value of being aligned with the United States. They are asking whether America will be there when it truly matters and whether the benefits are worth the tension with China. Here, Donald Trump is again not helping. By taking a crude and transactional approach to sharing the burden of security and a blunt approach to competition with China, Trump is damaging these relationships at the worst possible time. But Trump has sown something even more corrosive in the minds of many in the region: a mistrust of America's democracy and where it is heading. How can it have produced a leader who actively seeks to disrupt the very order that the United States built and benefited from? American reliability is tied up in whether the United States can turn itself around at home. US foreign policy will have to be backed by resources and a deep and enduring consensus within American society.

And yet this should be the golden era for US alliances in the Asia-Pacific, precisely because of the need for collective action and the high stakes involved.

Given the challenges of capacity and political will within regional and international institutions such as ASEAN and the United Nations, the future of multilateralism will likely be more ad-hoc arrangements among like-minded states.

US policy in recent years has sought to involve its most capable allies, including Australia and Japan, in trilateral arrangements, and in the Quadrilateral Security Dialogue (the Quad) – a powerful but sometimes halting partnership that also includes India. These arrangements can enable action to defend freedom of navigation and maritime information-sharing, and can lead to far more robust coalitions. For example, in the digital domain, the collective power of these countries will make cooperation not just desirable but essential in the larger contest between democracy and authoritarianism.

How comprehensive will that ad-hoc cooperation be? As China's economic and military power increases, will the region's largest democracies seek to knit together a new liberal order that actively tries to defend liberal-democratic values and push back on coercive practices? Or will bilateral, transaction-based approaches prevail? These choices are not only for the United States. Clearly, however, without strong leadership in democracies and more multilateralism, China will have a much freer hand to bend the international order towards its authoritarian preferences.

In defence of democracies

As we move further into this century, the United States and its democratic allies must take a more competitive approach to upholding and defending liberal-democratic values in the Asia-Pacific and beyond. We need to create a democratic bulwark in the face of rising authoritarianism, not just with China.

China is seeking to shape global governance in illiberal directions. Its vision, as China scholar Melanie Hart notes, is "a system based on authoritarian governance principles in which nations negotiate issues bilaterally instead of following common rules and standards. From a liberal democratic perspective, if Beijing succeeds in bringing about that vision, the world will be less free, less prosperous, and less safe."

The region's democracies need to understand and accept the ideological dimensions of this competition and see our own collective advantage more clearly. Our values are our distinguishing feature. They underpin our long-term resiliency – making our governments more accountable to citizens. And they remain attractive to people around the world, from Hong Kong to Tehran, from Baghdad to Santiago, from Beirut to Damascus. The desire for greater individual freedom will

There is an intense ideological dimension to this competition

continue to generate tensions within authoritarian or corrupt states. More importantly, without sustained high-level US and coordinated international pressure to advance universal rights and democratic freedoms, authoritarian governments will only push the boundaries of control further. There is an intense ideological dimension to this competition that cannot be ignored. And while US strategies to shape democratic outcomes through force or otherwise have fallen short, especially in recent history, the United States has been successful in providing a stable and secure environment for a more democratic Asia to emerge. Shifts towards authoritarianism in places such as

Thailand and the Philippines do not overshadow a democratic and peaceful Japan, a prosperous and vigorous South Korea or a strong and globally capable Australia.

Defending democracy does not mean that US strategy should aim to change Beijing's fundamental political orientation (history has also shown that we are not good at this sort of thing). But without more rigorous cooperation and coordination with its fellow democracies, China will step in to shape the order it wants at our expense. It is therefore imperative that we act to preserve our way of life and our personal freedoms, ensuring that democracy in Asia does not contract further and proving that might does not become right. This will require collective action among the region's democracies to preserve personal freedom of expression in the digital domain, to generate greater economic balance in relation to China, and to uphold the rule of law and push for the peaceful resolution of international disputes.

Regardless of whether Trump wins or loses the election on 3 November, the changing security, economic and political dynamics in the region, and the tough questions they give rise to, will continue to loom over US policymakers and allies. They will need to be addressed. And, crucially, the United States and its allies will need to address them together, and to define a common vision of an Asia-Pacific in which their values and prosperity can withstand changes to the existing order, now and into the future. ■

THE FIX
Solving Australia's foreign affairs challenges

—

John Blaxland on Developing a Grand Compact for the Pacific

"Australia could gain economically and politically from bolstering security and stability in the region, while also helping to limit destabilising external interference."

....

THE PROBLEM: The micro states of the Pacific are facing a range of existential challenges. These include: looming environmental catastrophe associated with climate change; inadequate governance; and maritime, territorial and domestic security problems related to or exacerbated by tensions between great powers battling for supremacy in the region. Many of these nations are ill-prepared for the likely consequences and have limited capacity to respond to them. Visionary and respectful Australian engagement is needed to avert disaster.

The South Pacific has long been treated as a policy backwater in Canberra, seen as Australia's (and New Zealand's) strategic safe space – the small nations there have been taken for granted, in part because they are politically oriented towards their larger Commonwealth neighbours. At the time of Australia's federation, much of the Pacific consisted of British colonies. Post-independence, these states retained a legacy of the English language and common law that left them with a system of governance most similar to those of Australia and New Zealand. Today, Australia and New Zealand are the first choices for education and alternative residence for many in the Pacific.

While proud of their distinctive cultures and political independence, the small Pacific states value the aid and support of Australia and New Zealand. But they resent Australia's unwillingness to lead more actively in addressing the risks of environmental disaster. Their small populations and economies also belie the enormous potential bestowed on them by the 1982 United Nations Convention on the Law of the Sea (UNCLOS), which has left them with exclusive economic zones (EEZs) that, cumulatively, are far larger and potentially more lucrative than those of many more-populous countries. Consequently, these states are subject to predatory behaviour from countries such as China.

During World War II, the South Pacific was fought over intensely, with US forces defending it as part of a strategy to keep sea-based communication lines open. Today it is difficult to envisage conflict on that scale, but the contest over the region's lucrative fisheries and potential seabed mineral resources is growing. As such supplies become scarce elsewhere in the world, greater competition is likely.

Recent Chinese generosity towards the smaller Pacific states – particularly the provision of development loans for infrastructure projects of dubious viability – have generated concern in the West. These loans can lead to excessive debt that gives China influence, if not control, over small and relatively vulnerable island communities.

This all presents a growing crisis, but also an opportunity. Many in the region are open to respectful and collegial Australian engagement and leadership, but suspicious of its waxing and waning of enthusiasm for all things Pacific. The federal government's "Pacific step-up" is a move in the right direction. But to protect Australia's long-term interests in the Pacific, something more substantive and far-reaching is needed.

THE PROPOSAL: Australia should offer a compact of association with South Pacific countries, allowing for shared governance. This would be akin to the treaty arrangements the United States has in the Pacific with Palau, the Marshall Islands and the Federated States of Micronesia, and New Zealand has with Niue and the Cook Islands.

The compact should come with an offer of residency (and potentially citizenship) for the population should the situation become untenable in their home islands. It should involve closer partnership arrangements over territorial and maritime domains, assisting with administration and management, security and governance – areas in which Australia already has capacity, expertise and experience.

To develop this compact, Australia should look to other Pacific arrangements as precedents, mindful of the need to tailor provisions to the requirements of individual nations. The compact should be offered to:

- Kiribati (population 115,000; EEZ 3.4 million square kilometres)
- Tonga (population 107,000; EEZ 660,000 square kilometres)
- Tuvalu (population 11,000; EEZ 750,000 square kilometres)
- Nauru (population 11,000; EEZ 308,000 square kilometres).

That means Australia would offer residency rights, and potentially citizenship, to just over 244,000 people, and help to administer and guarantee sovereignty to a cumulative EEZ of over 5.118 million square kilometres. Australia could gain economically and politically from bolstering security and stability in the region, while also helping to limit destabilising external interference.

Australia's former prime minister Kevin Rudd was recently criticised for proposing something similar: his "formal constitutional condominium" triggered an angry reaction from Tuvalu's prime minister, Enele Sopoaga, who accused Rudd of "imperialist thinking". But Sopoaga's criticisms are superficial. His remarks point to concerns over current policy regarding climate change – something that stronger domestic action could ameliorate. The proposal outlined here is a compact that is practical, respectful, inclusive and voluntary.

Such an arrangement makes sense for the smallest Pacific states because they have limited populations and resources to sustain effective international representation – in particular, to assert their rights and obligations under UNCLOS. The larger Pacific states have greater capacity to address these concerns. Still, a similar but less all-encompassing supportive arrangement could also be considered for the larger Pacific states, including:

- Vanuatu (population 270,000; EEZ 663,000 square kilometres)
- Solomon Islands (population 600,000; EEZ 1.59 million square kilometres)
- Fiji (population 898,000; EEZ 1.282 million square kilometres).

This could include more collaborative patrolling of EEZs – Royal Australian Navy vessel patrols supporting the local authorities – and some additional opportunities for residency in Australia.

Papua New Guinea, with a population of more than eight million and an EEZ of 2.402 million square kilometres, is in a league alone; it is large enough to sustain the economic and administrative burden of managing its own EEZ, and is too populous to expect residency rights for its citizens. Still, Australia should also look to bolster ties and deepen reciprocal arrangements with the nation, particularly around policing and related domestic governance issues.

WHY IT WILL WORK: Australia already invests heavily in bolstering governance, security, stability and prosperity in the Pacific. The Pacific step-up encompasses not just the seasonal worker program (involving nearly 30,000 Pacific Islanders) but also scholarships, infrastructure investment, climate and disaster resilience funding, a new patrol-boat and aerial surveillance program, and police and defence partnerships. There is already much cooperation over law enforcement, and legal and administrative arrangements. This suggests greater collaboration through a compact would be workable, if local sensitivities and cultural idiosyncrasies are taken into account.

Australia has a demand for additional workers. As a nation of migrants that benefits enormously from its multicultural composition, it has the capacity to absorb a surge in population from the Pacific. As part of the compact, Pacific citizens could also be encouraged to serve in Australian military and police forces.

Annually, Australia's net migration is about 200,000 people. Opening up residency opportunities to 244,000 more would likely only result in a small additional number of migrants over a span of years. Understandably, most islanders would prefer not to move; but under a compact, in the face of environmental or economic imperatives, they would have the freedom to choose. Those keenest to relocate could be among the first offered residency.

Some Australians might baulk at the costs of such a scheme, but in the long run the benefits – particularly the prospect of greater peace, security and stability in the Pacific – would outweigh the expense.

The success of a free compact arrangement will depend on presenting it in a respectful manner that considers Pacific environmental sensibilities. It will work only if Australia avoids a patronising, domineering and selfish approach, and agrees to safeguards that ensure the dignity of the states involved. It will be critical to articulate the mutual benefits, lest the arrangement appear a neo-colonial land grab. It should be presented as a multigenerational collaborative commitment.

This model of engagement should be pursued not just because of shared interests but as a generous-spirited attempt to find a solution to the problems Pacific micro-states face. The confluence of great-power contestation, governance challenges and looming environmental catastrophe points to the need for a concerted visionary response – and a grand compact of association for the Pacific is the most viable answer.

THE RESPONSE: The Department of Foreign Affairs and Trade said it was deepening engagement across the Pacific but would not say whether it supported or rejected offering countries a compact of association. It said it was enhancing economic and security ties through schemes such as the seasonal worker program and a program to support maritime patrols and surveillance. "We are listening and responding to the priorities identified by our Pacific partners to help address long-term security, economic and development challenges," a spokesperson said. "The government acknowledges the important contribution experts from academia and think tanks make in the policy development process via their contributions to discussion and debate." ■

Reviews

The Education of an Idealist: A Memoir
Samantha Power
William Collins

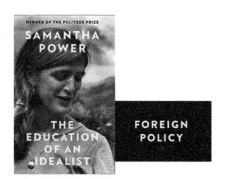

Samantha Power's time in President Obama's administration, first in the National Security Council and then as her country's representative at the United Nations in New York, overlapped almost entirely with the years I spent as administrator of the United Nations Development Programme, when I was particularly focused on international events. The topics covered in her memoir were highly familiar to me, but I found its insider's perspectives both insightful and refreshingly frank. I couldn't put this book down.

While Power subtitled her book "A Memoir", in reality it is an autobiography covering the first forty-seven years of her event-filled life. Her description of her childhood in Ireland, growing up with an alcoholic father, is heart-rending. In many ways the heroine of the book is her mother, who had the courage to take Samantha and her brother to the United States to begin a new life. There Samantha excelled in academia and sports, emerging from college with a deep interest in international affairs and a strong desire to make a difference.

The first vehicle she chose for that was journalism, becoming a correspondent in war-torn Bosnia, advocating for greater US attention to the conflict, and highlighting the impact of it on Bosnia's people. She then studied law at Harvard, with a view to gaining the skills to prosecute war criminals. She taught at the institution's John F. Kennedy School of Government and in 2003 won the Pulitzer Prize for Nonfiction for *A Problem from Hell: America and the Age of Genocide*, looking at why her adopted country had failed to respond to particular genocides.

Power's search for how she might make a greater contribution to human rights led her to engage with then senator Barack Obama in 2005. She spent some time on his staff and threw herself into his election campaign. In his first term in office, she became a senior political appointee, and subsequently was appointed a member of Cabinet and the US Permanent Representative at the United Nations.

This book emphasises that Power's voice in the administration was one of many, and rarely the dominant one. She often lacked regular direct access to the president, particularly in his first term. Representations she made on issues about which she felt passionately had to be delivered opportunistically, and weren't always welcomed by the president or his senior staff.

The meaning of the book's title may well have its origins in that period. Power staked her own reputation on Obama's 2008 campaign pledge that he would recognise the tragic events in Armenia in 1915 as a genocide. He did not. Even as a senior National Security Council official, Power was regularly blocked from travelling. Yet she succeeded in having the administration take on human rights, including rights for LGBTQIA people, and the prevention of mass atrocities as foreign policy priorities. Despite having to deal in the real world of intergovernmental haggling and positioning, there is no sign that Power ever resiled from her ideals. Those strong convictions, coupled with a willingness to settle for doing what she could when she could, and working with whomever she needed to, stood Power in good stead in her almost three and a half years as a member of Cabinet and an ambassador to the United Nations.

The work of the Security Council was her primary focus, but she also made it her business to meet almost every other ambassador there in their permanent missions to learn more about their perspectives and contexts. Her most important relationship in New York was undoubtedly with Vitaly Churkin, the Russian ambassador. One gains the impression that he went as far as he could within the confines of his instructions to find ways to move forward on a range of issues. In the aftermath of Obama's decision not to act when the Syrian regime crossed his red line on using chemical weapons, a decision with which Power disagreed, she worked successfully with Ambassador Churkin to craft an agreement at the Security Council on dismantling Syria's chemical weapons capacity.

The account of these years at the United Nations has some surprising omissions. It covers the very effective US response to the devastating Ebola outbreak in West Africa and the passage of the Security Council Resolution declaring Ebola a threat to international peace and security. Yet there is no mention of the United Nations Mission for Ebola Emergency Response, established with strong backing from the United States, which streamlined the work of United Nations agencies in the affected countries.

Similarly, there is silence on the United States' significant decision, in December 2016, to abstain on Security Council Resolution 2234 on Israeli settlements in "Palestinian territories occupied since 1967, including East Jerusalem". The resolution condemned the settlement activity as a flagrant violation of international law.

It demanded that Israel stop such activity and fulfil its obligations under international law as an occupying power. It was rare for the United States not to veto such a resolution.

The selection of a new UN secretary-general took place on Ambassador Power's watch. The process merits only two paragraphs in this 552-page text – perhaps unconsciously conveying how little significance the decision had for the United States. One is left with the overall impression that the United Nations was seen by even this relatively well-disposed administration as a platform for advocacy, but from which little concrete action was expected.

Such limitations aside, I read this book with a sense of nostalgia for a time when people of principle, such as Power, occupied senior positions in the US administration, and when there was a president who would consider a range of advice and deliberate carefully before making a decision. That is a far cry from today's Oval Office, from which tweet tirades signal daily mood switches, and where free and frank advice is neither welcomed nor heard.

That is what makes this book essential reading. It enables one to compare and contrast the circumstances of early 2020 with those of an era that is barely three years past, yet which seems like an eternity ago.

It is, however, in the nature of a pendulum to swing, and one fully expects that of the United States' foreign policy in future. This book convinces me that Power should play a role in that, and that there are many chapters yet to be written in the autobiography of this remarkable woman.

Helen Clark

Secret: The Making of Australia's Security State
Brian Toohey
Melbourne University Publishing

I n June 2019, the Australian Federal Police executed search warrants on the Sydney office of the ABC and the Canberra home of a NewsCorp journalist, creating headlines across Australia and around the world. The ensuing coverage has created a national debate about security and the media, including press freedom; initiatives such as Australia's Right to Know coalition; and a parliamentary inquiry into the "impact of the exercise of law enforcement and intelligence powers on the freedom of the press". The "raids" related to two separate police investigations from 2017 and 2018 into the unauthorised leaking and publishing of national security material.

In the midst of this intense focus on the nature of security in Australia and the role of the press comes veteran journalist Brian Toohey's *Secret*.

Toohey is no newcomer to issues around press leaks and national security. He is arguably best known for his work in the 1970s, reporting on and publishing leaked classified information about the role of the joint Australian–US defence facilities at North West Cape and Pine Gap. He is also known for co-authoring *Oyster: The Story of the Australian Secret Intelligence Service* (1989), which was subject to legal action over the alleged unauthorised disclosure of information related to national security.

Revelations around the Joint Defence Facility at Pine Gap and Naval Communication Station Harold E. Holt at North West Cape continue to compel Toohey. They also provide the two key arguments of his book.

The first is that Australia is a willing and naive pawn in the US "military-industrial-intelligence complex", and that this willingness has been nurtured by a small group of conservative politicians, military officials and bureaucrats. Special mention is made of Sir Arthur Tange, secretary of the Department of External Affairs and the Department of Defence in the 1960s, and Sir Charles Spry, the longtime head of the Australian Security Intelligence Organisation (ASIO). Toohey describes both as "addicted to secrecy". He suggests that others in more recent times have become unwittingly enamoured of secrecy in the relationship with the United States while remaining blind to Washington's motivations. In relation to Kim Beazley, the governor of Western Australia and a former defence minister and ambassador to the United States, Toohey comments that "secrets can be seductive – and deceptive".

The book's second argument is that these secrecy-obsessed individuals and their organisations have hidden vital information from the Australian people and even from the government. Toohey claims there is no need to withhold information about matters of national security, as history has shown that the perceived threats often prove unfounded, and that classified documents can be released without harm. To support his thesis, he lists a range of examples – for one, that the end of the Cold War and the demise of the Communist Party of Australia means that communism and its state sponsors, particularly the Soviet Union, never posed a serious threat.

Yet Toohey's arguments are weakened by his reluctance to give serious consideration to countervailing evidence, including recent revelations from archives. For instance, John Blaxland's official history of ASIO examines Toohey's assertions about US interference in Australian politics in the 1970s and concludes that nothing in ASIO's records – to which Blaxland had unimpeded access – supports the claims. Toohey dismisses this by stating that it must mean ASIO had not been told either, as Defence was in charge of the facility – despite Blaxland's findings being drawn from inquiries looking across government.

Contemporary security issues are treated with similar disdain. Toohey states that the 2019 Christchurch mosque shootings could have been prevented if Australian agencies had shared relevant information with their New Zealand counterparts – but there is no evidence that authorities had credible information about an impending terrorist attack. Russia is exonerated of any responsibility for the poisoning of Sergei and Yulia Skripal in the United Kingdom, despite charges being laid against Russian officials; Toohey states that

the chemicals could have come from elsewhere, and that if Putin wanted to murder Skripal, "it would have been cheaper and safer to shoot him with an untraceable gun". The rhetoric of national security, according to Toohey, is a convenient way to control information in the interests of power and politics, and to cover up the "shoddy" work of politicians and some senior officials. This politicised perspective is understandable from someone who spent his career in the press gallery, but it fails to account for the confidentiality and security requirements of modern militaries and governments.

It is in the discussion of the Whitlam era that *Secret* shines. Toohey homes in on the Whitlam government's attempts to fulfil its election promise to find out about, and make public, the role of the joint Australian–US facilities. Whitlam emerges as a champion of free speech and responsible government, dogged and undermined by Tange and others, who were deeply suspicious of the new, left-leaning government and concerned that it could undermine Australia's alliance with the United States (which at the time was led by Richard Nixon). Recounting a closed-door meeting in 1972 between a US congressman and the soon-to-be Whitlam government defence minister Lance Barnard, Toohey presents a contrast between Barnard saying "whatever the Americans wanted to hear" on Pine Gap, and himself stepping up – in his position then as a Labor staffer – to clarify the nuances of the new Whitlam government's views. In a chapter titled "Dangerous Advice from Ignorant Officials", Toohey blames Tange for convincing Whitlam to break his election commitment. The dark hand of the United States looms in the background, with a suggestion – no direct accusation – that it may have had a role in the dismissal of the Whitlam government. "Kerr was our man", a shady former CIA Canberra station chief later confided to Toohey over lunch in Washington.

The account of the Whitlam and Fraser years also provides revealing insights into the political players of the time. In the 1970s and 1980s, in the cramped and bustling halls of Old Parliament House, journalists worked cheek-by-jowl with their political colleagues, and did the morning rounds by visiting ministers in their offices to share a cigarette and perhaps a drink. Toohey mentions Minister for Defence James Killen, seen by many journalists as a "wit and a bon vivant". These chapters are full of references to many leaks of information that had been circulated to "small numbers of ministers", with officials reportedly often "unfazed" by the leaks. Today, the federal parliamentary press gallery is in a wing on the Senate side of the vast Parliament House complex. If a politician wants to meet with journalists, there's a long walk involved; more often, media advisers stroll the gallery and use press conferences and media releases to get the message out. Toohey's anecdotes – both his own remembrances and those he relates from others – speak to a bygone intimacy between politicians and members of the fourth estate. When Justice Robert Hope was appointed to investigate a leak involving then defence minister Bill Hayden, Toohey observes drily that Hope "looked a little surprised to see me coming in Hayden's door as he was leaving", and that Hayden had immediately told him what Hope had said. What shines through is a deep familiarity with the personalities and issues of the day (Toohey was also briefly an opposition ministerial press secretary), making *Secret* a valuable addition to our understanding of the politics of the time.

This focus gives context to the leaks Toohey was involved with – and highlights starkly the contrast with leaks from today. Toohey's recollections of the relative ease of picking up and handing on papers, and the almost unimpeded access to ministers and their offices, is a world away from contemporary allegations that officials with security clearances downloaded documents illegally from classified IT systems and removed them clandestinely from secure premises.

Secret is a curious book. Part memoir and part extended op-ed, it explores a wide range of themes and events. In sixty chapters over 330 pages, Toohey gives his views on Australian politics, security and defence; the two world wars and the Vietnam War; the West's approach to Putin's Russia (the United States is blamed for tensions with Russia); the rise of China, India and Indonesia; and nuclear testing and biological weapons. Yet despite its title, it is not a researched history of Australia's security apparatus, or even focused

primarily on press freedom and security.

This is a pity, as it means Toohey misses two important opportunities. The first is to educate readers about the important relationship between the national security and defence community, and the media. The second is to promote his views about the limitations on press freedom to those in a position to bring about change. There is an appetite in Australia, particularly at the moment, for addressing and discussing public access to official information. But the book risks putting some readers off due to its oversimplification of complex matters, its anti-US conspiracy theories and its tendency to represent police, security and defence personnel as Keystone Cops.

However, for those actively engaged in the debate about press freedom, *Secret* is worth reading for one important reason: it provides insight into the way national security is perceived by the media and some of the public. The book highlights the importance for liberal democracies such as Australia to not only enhance public and legal accountability, and engage in a constructive dialogue with the populace, but to emphatically be seen to be doing so.

The current inquiry by the Parliamentary Joint Committee on Intelligence and Security has borne this out: submissions from media organisations indicate a widespread belief that security classifications are applied to documents randomly, and that there is no effective form of accountability other than the media and whistleblowers. The inquiry has also shown that there is limited public understanding of the risks in releasing classified information.

Information on Australia's national security agencies and how they work is often lacking or oversimplified. Public understanding could be enhanced by explaining, for example, the long-established protocols around classification and handling of materials, and the reasons for these measures, along with how Australia's security laws work, and how and why they have been reviewed and amended over the years. Good information is publicly available, but it is often buried in *Hansard*, in annual reports or on departmental websites, where few would seek it out.

It is incumbent on security and defence officials to provide more accessible information on these topics. As we are currently seeing, a failure to do so leads to misapprehension of what the government and the security and defence establishments are doing, and why.

Secret is a reminder of the importance of informed debate, and the role of frank and fearless journalism – and opinion – in helping it along. While the book is not a comprehensive reference on the history of security in Australia, there is utility of a different kind in hearing directly from someone who witnessed so many key events in Australia's history up close, in proximity to political leaders, at a time when it was still possible to do so. One can almost smell the worn leather armchairs of the parliamentary offices and hear the clacking typewriters of the old press gallery. Keeping secrets – and leaking them – was different back then.

Jacinta Carroll

Malevolent Republic:
A Short History of
the New India
K.S. Komireddi
Hurst

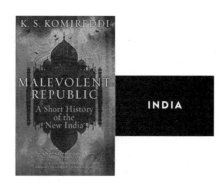

Twelve years ago, I was sitting in a Shanghai auditorium, waiting to take the stage for a discussion of matters literary. The speaker preceding me was the Indian novelist – and, by then, polemicist – Arundhati Roy.

Roy has a beautiful voice, the kind that makes you want to close your eyes and just listen to her cadences. So I did. But her speech was disturbing. She spoke of political horrors so extreme you would have thought her topic was Nazi Germany. Yet she was speaking about the world's largest democracy, India.

Recently, reading Kapil Satish Komireddi's debut book-length polemic *Malevolent Republic: A Short History of the New India*, I was reminded of that moment in Shanghai when a renowned Indian author seemed to me to lose perspective. But then, I am also reminded of Nobel Laureate Amartya Sen's celebration of the "argumentative Indian", and his vision of India as an ongoing religious, political and economic arm-wrestle.

Komireddi's strident book appears in the wake of last year's historic election victory for Prime Minister Narendra Modi and his Bharatiya Janata Party (BJP). The Congress Party – which secured India's independence in 1947 under the leadership of Jawaharlal Nehru and the cajoling of Mahatma Gandhi – was shattered by its worst ever electoral performance, gaining less than 20 per cent of the national vote. For Komireddi, the result was both regrettable and inevitable, a logical outcome of decades of the Congress Party's corruption, dynastic rule and betrayal of India's secular foundations for short-term political gain. However, it is the Hindu nationalist BJP, and Modi in particular, who cop the brunt of the author's ire.

Komireddi's central thesis is that India is undergoing a creeping, bottom-up political and cultural revolution that could conceivably bring about a Hindu nation-state, a mirror image of Pakistan, in which 200 million Indian Muslims end up as second-class citizens. Unfortunately, recent events – most notably, the introduction of a discriminatory citizenship law that sparked clashes between demonstrators and police – lend credibility to what might otherwise have been dismissed as a fevered, far-left fantasy.

In his first term, the energetic Mr Modi reached out to the world, including India's near neighbours, blunting fears he would pursue a sectarian agenda. But in August 2019, the Modi government took the extraordinary step of revoking the limited autonomy granted under Article 370 of the Indian constitution to the state of Jammu and Kashmir, and cut lines of communication within the Muslim-majority Kashmir Valley. Hindu nationalists cheered. Then, in November, the Supreme Court ruled that the long-disputed religious site at Ayodhya, in India's most populous state of Uttar Pradesh, would be handed to a trust that will construct a Hindu temple on the ruins of a Muslim shrine destroyed by a Hindu mob in 1992. The hoodlums guilty of that crime – which I was there to witness – have never been brought to justice.

In days gone by, such a ruling would have triggered an immediate backlash from the Congress, but the party is now deeply divided, as is the broader polity after decades of caste-based politics. Komireddi writes, "India's tragedy is that just when it is faced with an existential crisis, there exists no pan-Indian alternative to the BJP ... The values of Hindu nationalism have become the default setting of Indian politics." He portrays Indian corporates as fawning lackeys of Modi and claims that respected institutions, including the Election Commission of India, the Reserve Bank of India, the judiciary and even the military, have been cowed into silence, unwilling or unable to defend the country's secular constitution. And he quotes social theorist Ashis Nandy, who once interviewed Modi, describing the current leader of the world's largest democracy as "a fascist and a prospective killer, perhaps even a future mass murderer".

At times, Komireddi's hyperbole gets the better of his analysis, but he writes with insight, passion and an arresting vocabulary of rarely used words, spoilt by almost as many typos. For this reader, *Malevolent Republic* is most persuasive when it details Modi's numerous policy missteps: the bungled and ill-considered abolition of small-denomination rupee banknotes; the short-lived rapprochement with India's neighbours that quickly turned into a series of nasty spats, including a tense military standoff with China in Sikkim in 2017; the bullying of landlocked Nepal that served only to strengthen pro-China sentiment there; and a confused and confusing carbon reduction strategy.

According to news magazine *India Today*, unemployment is at a forty-year high of 6 per cent, while the Press Trust of India reports that direct foreign investment actually declined in 2019 to a six-year low. The economy is still growing at 7 per cent annually, but observers warn that the potential demographic dividend of a young population may evaporate unless policymakers

respond better to local conditions in the country's twenty-nine states. If they don't, young voters inspired by Modi could quickly become disillusioned with him.

There are, then, two Narendra Modis in *Malevolent Republic*. One is an incompetent Dr Jekyll, ruling via a series of ill-considered thought bubbles; the other an evil Mr Hyde spurred by religious nationalism.

Both are plausible, but can they simultaneously be true? And if not, which is the real Modi? Unfortunately, it is a question the author neither asks nor answers.

Indians frustrated with corruption and inefficiency have long dreamt of a messiah who will drag the country forward. Partition-era squabbles over Kashmir and Ayodhya are indeed costly and distracting. Yet for Komireddi, Modi's sectarianism – his blind eye to the violence of Hindu mobs – will make India less just, more divided along ethnic and religious lines, and dangerously at odds with its neighbours.

In 2014, Sanjaya Baru, a journalist and former media adviser to outgoing prime minister Dr Manmohan Singh, commented that Modi's rise to power heralded the birth of a second Indian republic. Komireddi cites Baru's observation that "our nation's first phase of being a republic lasted from 1950 to 2014, the second phase has begun". Interpreting this comment, Komireddi adds, "He [Baru] meant that the India founded in 1947 by Congress was dead."

Modi's ascendancy may not continue. Voters will punish any sign of hubris or incompetence. But things that were once unthinkable in India are now happening, lending an air of prophecy to Komireddi's grim observations that "we inhabit the most degraded moment in the history of the Indian Republic" and "if a temple rises on the site of the Babri mosque, it will be as a tombstone for the secular state".

Modi's second term is less than a year old, but it is already looking very different from his first. The second Indian republic beckons.

Christopher Kremmer

Correspondence

"History Hasn't Ended"
by Allan Gyngell

David Brophy

In his essay "History Hasn't Ended" (AFA7: *China Dependence*), Allan Gyngell writes that China's rise is testing the "sensible centrist consensus" that has long prevailed among Australia's foreign policy establishment. He wants to defend that consensus and make the case for "foreign policy" as the remedy for Australia's China-induced anxieties.

The thing about foreign policy, though, is that those sitting at the table tend to keep their cards close to their chests. A country's actual foreign policy, its negotiating points and red lines, and its view of other parties' interests and intentions, are not always things to be aired publicly.

That's been the case for some time now, as Australian politicians insist, against mounting odds, that "we won't have to choose" between China and the United States. Gyngell's article is a sophisticated restatement of that orthodoxy, and exhibits some of its inherent ambiguities.

Gyngell declares his stance towards the essay's conclusion: "China will be the most powerful state in the region." But he has chosen his words carefully: *in the region*. He is agnostic as to whether this entails an end to US hegemony in Asia – "The United States may no longer be the regional hegemon," he notes. It's a possibility, but no certainty.

China and the United States might continue their economic estrangement and settle in for a Cold War, or they might not. But Gyngell's scenario for US–China reconciliation strikes me as implausible. Its first element is that China will decide to accommodate "the security and economic anxieties of its partners". Assuming these "partners" include the United States, just how likely is it that Beijing will reconcile itself to Washington's expansive view of its security interests in Asia? Can we really expect China to abandon efforts to cultivate globally competitive champions such as Huawei?

The second element of this scenario is that "the United States will resolve the current dysfunction of its government and accommodate itself to a more multipolar world". But this gets things back to front. To the extent that the United States has been willing to accommodate multipolarity in recent times, it's been *because* of its dysfunction. It sometimes feels as if Donald Trump's inconsistency is the only thing standing between Washington and an all-out containment policy on China.

If the only way out of an incipient Cold War is for China to voluntarily step back from the confrontation, or for the United States to drop its determination to prevent the emergence of regional rivals, Australia may well end up disappointed.

It's not surprising, then, that an alternative, more hawkish position has been gaining ground of late. In contrast to Gyngell's picture of a gradual evolution, these people see US–China relations as on a collision course, and contemplate measures to ensure that the United States and its allies emerge victorious. Their worry is that US hegemony in Asia might be more important to Australia than it is to the United States itself, and so the sub-imperial reflex – to step up and stiffen Washington's resolve – has kicked in.

Gyngell is quite right to criticise alarmist talk of Chinese subversion, which has helped to turn public opinion and to advertise Australia's "front line" role in combating China to its allies. But as he also points out, the talk is having the desired effect. And it's not all made up, either: what Beijing is doing to the Uighurs in Xinjiang, for example, is truly shocking.

Dovish voices can always point to the economic benefits of engagement with China. But those benefits have been far from evenly distributed: the lion's share has gone to foreign-owned resource giants. It's nice to think that doing business with China "provides us with more opportunities to build a just society". But in practice, the China boom has done nothing to reduce Australian inequality. The example of anti-Japanese sentiment in the late 1980s tells us that ordinary people's economic vulnerabilities can just as easily be mobilised in the interests of China-bashing as in support of an elite "engagement" strategy.

If, as I think is likely, trends in US–China relations prove the optimists wrong, the sensible centrist consensus that Australia "won't have to choose" will find itself on shaky ground. Other elements of that consensus can easily be put to the service of a more partisan policy: the belief that US hegemony has delivered the best of possible worlds, for example, or that certain "values" endow Western foreign policy with a moral mission that Beijing's lacks. A more defensible and complete response to Australia's China panic has to extend to a critique of these tenets too.

David Brophy is a senior lecturer in modern Chinese history
at the University of Sydney

Jane Orton

In "History Hasn't Ended", Allan Gyngell proposes that "there is no Australian future in which China will not be central". This means, he says, that "we have to manage a relationship with a country so different in its language, culture, history and values" and "understand China in all its complexity" in order to "engage with it as it is". Just a couple of lines later, he points out our shortcomings that make this approach difficult: serious national inadequacies in China experience, socio-political expertise and language proficiency. Gyngell does not aim, in his essay, to elaborate on solutions to these. But I am concerned that he does not acknowledge that the critical base for any genuinely expert knowledge and deep understanding of China, and for developing the resilient relationships he suggests we need, must be a solid percentage of Australians proficient in Chinese.

The future Gyngell advocates for Australia requires being able to communicate, cooperate and compete internationally in a China-centred region. To do this, we must be able to independently source and judge information from China that is central to our interests. In order to build strong, loyal partnerships, Australian government agencies, companies, educational and cultural bodies, small businesses and hospitality organisations all need to be informed of the other party's needs and preferences and of its social and political environment. There are very clear limitations if we can only conduct most of our engagement with China by relying on English.

Failing to expand our long-term linguistic capacities discourages the evolving national self-image that Gyngell proposes and instead allows the majority of Australians to remain trapped in a colonial mindset, seeing English as the only language of engagement. This leaves them passively reliant on what Chinese speakers can or choose to tell them. Monolingual Australians are often unaware that the excellent formal English of paid translators may mask a shallow understanding of their field, or that Chinese-Australian colleagues who sound fluent may not have developed their language skills to working adult standards.

As well, communicating through translators is awkward, and makes it difficult to build the relationships of mutual understanding and trust we need to form new means of cooperation. The responsibility for creating such relationships must be broadly spread, not left just to Chinese-Australians – at 5.6 per cent of the population, there are far too few of them. The deep, long-lasting engagement with China that Gyngell proposes needs to be undertaken by many more Australians, from all walks of life.

Language proficiency should be raised early in conjunction with any policy proposals because it requires long-term planning and ongoing support. It is far too late for students to begin encountering Chinese language at university if the aim is to have graduates who can confidently and competently understand spoken and written Chinese in their professional fields. In literacy alone, this would mean knowing some 4000 characters.

At present, Australian Year 12 students of Chinese language from non-Chinese backgrounds enter university knowing a scant 500 characters. That is Grade 1 level literacy in Chinese societies, where students graduate from high school having learned 6000 characters. In any case, at present there are only some 2400 students nationally who are taking Year 12 Chinese, of whom fewer than 350 are from non-Chinese backgrounds. In Victoria, where half of these Chinese-language students live, the number from non-Chinese backgrounds has decreased by 23 per cent in the last three years. Not all who take Year 12 Chinese continue with the language at university, and of those who do, few persist with it for more than a year after they enter tertiary education. The shortfall in competence is enormous, and cannot be redressed quickly.

The only chance for any local university graduate to reach a level of Chinese proficiency adequate for professional engagement is to begin studying the language in early primary school and continuing with it in secondary school, learning Chinese in a high-frequency, intensive program (five to ten hours per week), ideally by studying something substantive from the regular curriculum. This would provide content interesting enough that students want to persevere, and offer enough language by their early years of secondary school for them to be working competently in science and the humanities using Chinese. Such a program, complemented by solid studies in English, would develop competent dual-language speakers and writers by the point of tertiary entrance.

Moving from the comfort of an international world in which English has been the key into one where Chinese-language skills are a significant asset will be a crucial part of passing what Gyngell calls "this generation's great national test".

Jane Orton is a member of the Graduate School of Education at the University of Melbourne

Alison Broinowski

Since John Howard repelled refugees and committed Australia to the War on Terror in 2001, national security has dominated our foreign and defence policies – with the unquestioning consent of both major parties, like a wartime government of national unity. The "endless war", the longest in our history, has made Australia a fortress, barricaded by some eighty-five pieces of national security legislation. Most ministers and opposition spokespeople stay safely below the parapets.

Debate, however, is awakening. In December 2018 the Australian Labor Party agreed to hold an inquiry into the war powers that enable our successive troop commitments to the Middle East. Outgoing ambassador to the United States Joe Hockey recently told Americans what he thinks about US protectionism. Penny Wong has been critical of the Coalition for its lack of long-term planning. Many in the commentariat suggest we need a review of the 2017 Foreign Affairs White Paper (which was to have provided "philosophical guidance" to last a decade). The prime minister made positive points about Australia–China relations before his talks with President Trump, after which he backtracked, advocated "negative globalism" – presumably referring to the UN General Assembly – and challenged China's status as a developing country in the World Trade Organization. Foreign minister Marise Payne has since attacked China over human rights.

The timing could not be better for Allan Gyngell's fine essay on how (and how not) to handle China. With a distinguished record in government, academia and multiple think tanks, Gyngell is adept at defining the middle ground. As an author, he favours the practical over the theoretical, and the "sensible" over the radical. So he points not only to China's slowing rise and its internal challenges, but also to its justifiable ambitions. He recognises that despite falling Chinese investments, reduced commodity imports, and alleged interference in Australian institutions and universities, Australia's engagement with China must continue. Australia needs more expertise on China, he observes – but now that the "magic decades" of the relationship are over, funding for that will not be so easy to come by.

Thanks to Gyngell's even-handedness, "History Hasn't Ended" will not alarm Australian readers inside or outside the policy fortress. It might, if he admitted that our government's actions don't always match their advice to China. At America's urging, Australia has joined a revived Indo-Pacific Quadrilateral Security Dialogue, the Quad, which seeks encirclement and containment of China, inviting negative reactions from Beijing. Gyngell points to China's rejection of international tribunal rulings on the South China Sea, but not to Australia excluding itself from international maritime jurisdiction over East Timor. He doesn't say that while Australian forces are illegally deployed in the Middle East, China has adhered to the UN Charter and invaded no other country. He is concerned about Chinese cyber-hacking and cultivation of influential individuals, which any country – including Australia – does if it can. He shares the security agencies' concerns about Huawei as a keyhole into Australians' data – but as Edward Snowden revealed, the United States and its technology companies have collected everything for years. Gyngell wisely recommends more clarity about our current objectives, but this requires comparing the United States and its counterproductive military expeditions with China, which has peacefully attracted 152 states to sign on to its Belt and Road Initiative.

Despite his preference for practicality, Gyngell several times invokes differences of values, which he hopes China and Australia will manage for the good of the relationship. For Australia, he writes, these include human rights, free speech and the rule of law. A Chinese reader of Australia's self-redacted newspapers in late 2019 might wonder if the first two rights are guaranteed to Australians much more than they are to Chinese. Australian leaders' claims that nobody, environment protesters in particular, is above the law might also puzzle Chinese observers. Shared values? Peter Dutton wants facial recognition of all

Australians, which both China and Facebook can do – which is why face masks are banned in Hong Kong, and hoodies in Chile. But China has not invaded Syria and seized control of its oil, as Trump admits the United States has. Imagine the Australian reaction to China doing that! A distinguished colleague of Gyngell's says values are what leaders cite when they run out of other ways to differentiate between countries.

While Gyngell observes that foreign policy involves weighing up competing interests, it's clear that Australia favours our unreliable, incapable ally over our ambitious regional neighbour and largest trading partner. If we are to seek the middle ground Gyngell advocates, Australia should pay more attention to how our Asian and Pacific neighbours deal with China in a way that avoids confrontation. Instead, reverting to Sinophobia, Marise Payne and defence minister Linda Reynolds side with Trump.

We are missing the opportunity to engage with our region peacefully for the economic benefit of all. The Australia–China relationship, former ambassador to the People's Republic of China Geoff Raby said recently, is at its lowest point in our forty-six years of diplomatic relations. It may already be too late.

Alison Broinowski is a former Australian diplomat and academic

Luke Gosling

Allan Gyngell's essay is commendable for its even-keeled policy prescriptions and rare level-headed tone in discussing our complex and consequential relationship with China.

The China debate in Australia is becoming dominated by competing filters, as Gyngell points out. He warns that politicians voicing their thought bubbles can be outright damaging to the national interest. Our policy on China calls for bipartisanship and should be founded on sound foreign policy principles, not play to the populism of the day.

Across politics, government, academia and the media, many are commenting on China's internal and external behaviour using reheated ideological tropes. Some believe that Beijing's growing techno-authoritarian traits and Leninist roots make it an innate danger to everything we hold dear. But Cold War and Orwellian analogies are poor substitutes for critical thinking. We should not pre-emptively cast China only as a threat.

This recycled thinking is out of touch with the nuanced challenges that China's rise represents for Australia and the region. Framing China as alien to us unhelpfully ignores that Chinese strategists are students of Carl von Clausewitz as well as Sun Tzu. Even if they weren't, China is beholden to the same geopolitical constraints that have always applied to great powers.

The idea that China is acting or will act differently to other rising powers because of its political system or its culture is not supported by history. Yet this assumption is central to some who cast any form of diplomatic engagement with Beijing as panda-hugging and, ultimately, appeasement. Ironically, the same assumption feeds the narrative of Chinese propagandists and their apologists in the West, who argue that, by virtue of its uniqueness, China can only rise peacefully.

We can avoid these pitfalls by adopting a more realist, independent and balanced foreign policy posture, and not only in regard to China.

Realism means recalibrating our words to more honestly match our deeds. For instance, the government often takes credit for upholding the rules-based order, but engages in ham-fisted megaphone diplomacy and tactless sledging of multilateral institutions.

We should absolutely express our concerns on core values such as human rights, especially when there are deeply worrying reports of rights violations, as in China's mass detention of Uighurs. But to avoid being accused of double standards, we would need to be consistent by not remaining deafeningly silent when serious allegations concern important strategic partners other than China.

Too often, the government treats foreign policy like virtue-signalling. This is the only way to explain how cabinet ministers can think it helpful to repeatedly snipe at our largest trading partner where diplomatic channels would be far more effective.

This sniping needs to stop. We can learn from our neighbours. Some of our South-East Asian friends have managed to carefully and effectively balance bland public statements on the most sensitive issues in their relationships with China – including on territorial claims in the South China Sea – with pointed actions. This is more effective than conducting foreign policy by media release without commensurate action.

Realism also means recognising the limits of our relative power in the region and doing something about it. This was on Kevin Rudd's mind when he announced Australia's acquisition of twelve future submarines.

A more realist and independent Australian foreign policy is not about choosing between the United States and China. It's about choosing the path of all self-respecting middle powers and of every great power: self-reliance. A bigger, stronger, more independent Australia would more comfortably define and assert its interests independently of other Indo-Pacific or Western capitals, even if doing so could mean standing alone and without cover from our traditional allies.

Such a position would not pose a threat to our alliance with the United States, as some erroneously think. Being a "strategy maker" and not just a "strategy taker" in the region, to use former chief of the army Peter Leahy's useful distinction, would make us an even more valuable US ally.

Adopting a balanced foreign policy also means defining values we won't trade for interests – and core interests we won't trade for lesser interests. And it would mean realising that our values often compete. Gyngell reminds us that prosperity is a value too. So is peace, as Hugh White has written.

Foreign policy is a complex business, and so is our relationship with China. Both are only becoming more so. While a more realist, independent and balanced foreign policy would not end this complexity, it would make us more self-assured, more consistent and, ultimately, more successful at finding our identity and our sense of security within Asia.

Luke Gosling is the federal member for Solomon and chair of the Australian Labor Party's Indo-Pacific Trade Taskforce

Allan Gyngell responds

I am grateful to the respondents for engaging so thoughtfully with my essay. As China's centrality to the issues that matter to Australia grows, the scope and tone of the national debate will be vital. If Australia is to advance its interests and protect its values effectively, it is important that we acknowledge the complexity of the issues at stake. Great dangers lie ahead if our attitudes towards China are reduced to a badge of political identity.

That's one reason I am grateful to Luke Gosling, a member of parliament and former soldier, for his contribution. His call for realism in the debate is obviously one that resonates with me. Gosling hopes for bipartisanship on China policy. At the highest levels we've mostly had that, but the tough part comes when we drill down into what exactly his "more realist, independent and balanced" policy towards China might require. That's where the debate begins. It's important that he and other parliamentarians are part of it.

I agree with Jane Orton that if Australia is to achieve our objectives with China, we require a "solid percentage of Australians fluent in Chinese". With Daniel Kane, she was the source of the figure I quoted that only about 130 Australians of non-Chinese background are thought to be proficient enough in Chinese to conduct business at the highest levels. It's a shocking number, but RMIT ABC Fact Check confirmed it as an educated guess.

Hugh Aliprandi, a high-school Chinese-language teacher, wrote perceptively about this dilemma in his AFA Next Voices article, "Minding the Gaps":

> At the moment, Australians are playing on China's terms, unwilling to craft our own narrative, relying on translators and other people's

interpretations of the events unfolding in our neighbourhood. For better or worse, we are rushing headfirst into the twenty-first century, content so far to play the eternal guest.

The 1.2 million Australians of Chinese heritage will have an important role to play in our engagement with China, and we are underutilising their contribution. But as Orton indicates, it is lazy to imagine that we can outsource certain elements of the China–Australia relationship to that community. Even in less difficult tasks than learning a foreign language, Australians' general understanding of Chinese history and culture, both classical and contemporary, is depressingly inadequate to help us comprehend and deal with a country of such importance.

David Brophy is sceptical about my belief that greater recognition of the role of foreign policy will help manage the relationship. The thing about foreign policy, he writes, is that "those sitting at the table tend to keep their cards close to their chests". I think he is confusing foreign policy with diplomacy and its processes. Foreign policy is no more secret in its articulation and implementation than defence policy or economic policy. On the contrary, clarity and consistency in the way we deal with other governments is at its essence.

Brophy describes me as representing "a sophisticated restatement" of the orthodoxy that Australia won't have to choose between China and the United States. In fact, I have been critical of the use of that mantra by Australian political leaders. (One way of thinking about Australian foreign policy is to see it as a seventy-year-long effort to avoid hard choices.) Every day, Australian policymakers are making choices about how to respond and what to say on issues ranging from the South China Sea to the use of 5G technology. Foreign policy lies in those myriad choices.

But I concede that I have difficulty imagining circumstances short of catastrophic war in which the Chinese government issues an ultimatum – ditch the ANZUS Treaty or we cease buying your iron ore – or that we would capitulate if they did.

Brophy is more pessimistic than I am about the outcome of strategic competition between the United States and China. He may be right. It is certainly a grave danger that our defence planners need to consider. But my simple scenarios were not predictions. My point was that no matter what the future holds, Australia's relations with China will remain crucial, and our interests are not the same as those of the United States.

Alison Broinowski, Gosling and Brophy are right to ask for consistency in the way we respond to challenges to values, norms or laws. As Gosling writes, if we are "silent when serious allegations concern important strategic partners other than China, we risk being accused of double standards". Our concern about the treatment of Muslim minorities in Asia, for example, should apply equally to Chinese Uighurs, Rohingyas in Myanmar and Indian Muslims in Assam or Kashmir. If we weaponise our values in order to deploy them selectively for political ends, we have lost.

Of course, we should also act at home in ways consistent with our own values and laws. But I think Broinowski brushes aside too lightly real differences between Australia and China in the exercise of human rights, free speech and the rule of law.

Gosling and Broinowski say we can learn from our neighbours in South-East Asia. That's true at a broad level, but I'm not sure it gets us as far as they imagine. It's not possible in a democracy like ours to "manage" a complex relationship with China in the way Singapore can. Each of the countries of South-East Asia brings its own mix of historical experience and contemporary interests to its relationship with China, and ASEAN's difficulty in finding a common position on the South China Sea reflects this. Nevertheless, both respondents are right to call for a deep, continuous conversation with the region, exchanging views and developing ways of working together, including in the management of Chinese power. That, again, is the work of foreign policy.

I sense a slight disappointment in both Brophy's and Broinowski's responses with what Broinowski calls my "even-handedness". She describes me as "adept at defining the middle ground". As this is a discussion about China, I'll call to my defence the voice of Confucius, as imagined by Ezra Pound in *The Cantos*:

> Anyone can run to excesses,
> It is easy to shoot past the mark,
> It is hard to stand firm in the middle.

As any politician will tell you, the middle ground is where the battles are fought and won.

Allan Gyngell is national president of the Australian Institute of International Affairs and an honorary professor at the Australian National University

"High Price" by Margaret Simons

James Laurenceson

Universities are the vanguard of Australia's engagement with China. They sell education services to Chinese students. Their researchers collaborate extensively with Chinese colleagues. Some host Confucius Institutes, cross-cultural education organisations funded by China. At the University of Queensland, a serving Chinese diplomat has even been appointed to the faculty, albeit in an honorary (and unpaid) capacity.

As the geostrategic ground has shifted in recent years, this interaction, rather than being celebrated as in the national interest, has seen universities thrust into the spotlight of Australia's Chinese interference debate. The above examples are now regularly cited as avenues through which Australian sovereignty might be compromised.

Margaret Simons' article "High Price" (AFA7: *China Dependence*) delves into the risks stemming from Australian universities' exposure to the Chinese student dollar.

Simons' contribution achieves what much commentary on this topic does not. Alongside the risks, she recognises the benefits that Chinese students bring, such as underwriting Australia's research capacity. Simons also includes qualification from an expert, who states that only a "very tiny minority" of the more than 150,000 Chinese students in Australia are involved in activities that could be construed as threatening freedom of speech. And, she observes, "[t]he same couple of anecdotes tend to get recycled". Rather than just speculating *about* Chinese student views, Simons talks *with* students, revealing, among other things, a willingness to question Chinese government positions and a desire to be better integrated into Australian society.

In all this, Simons' analysis provides a model for how a productive discussion around risks of interference might proceed.

Consider research collaboration. Australian universities have been accused of partnering with China on work that boosts the capabilities of the People's Liberation Army. The broader context in which these allegations are made is overviewed in a July 2019 report I co-wrote with colleague Michael Zhou ("Partners in Knowledge Creation: Trends in Australia–China Research Collaboration and Future Challenges"). It suggests a more hopeful narrative. By one metric, China is on the cusp of becoming Australia's leading international partner in knowledge creation, an endeavour vital to Australia's prosperity. In technology-driven fields such as computer science and engineering, collaboration with China is now critical. For example, 71 per cent of Australia's most-cited articles on computer science in 2017 featured an author affiliated with a Chinese institution.

Despite this growth in research partnerships, one fact stands out: not a single example has been produced of a university evading the regulations put in place by the Australian government to mitigate national security risks, such as Defence Export Controls.

These controls include exemptions for "basic scientific research", defined as "experimental or theoretical work . . . not primarily directed towards a specific practical aim or objective". Such exemptions exist not out of generosity to universities but to protect against another risk: that of Australia being cut off from creating knowledge with partners across the globe, including China.

Controls in the United States feature a "fundamental research exclusion" that is even more wide-ranging. This applies to "basic and applied research in science and engineering where the resulting information is ordinarily published and shared broadly within the scientific community". Researchers in Australian universities are not in the business of keeping their methods, data and findings hidden. In fact, the opposite is true, given that the path to academic promotion is to publish or perish.

And even as the US Department of Commerce reviews whether controls should be extended to cover "emerging technologies" such as artificial intelligence, it has already stated it does not seek to expand its jurisdiction to include fundamental research.

The modest scale of Australia's research capacity means that US regulations cannot be used as a default local benchmark anyway.

There is a question to be asked about whether Defence Trade Controls remain fit for purpose in a changed national security environment featuring a China that is more assertive abroad and repressive at home. But this is precisely what prompted the government to commission an independent expert review in 2018. The review concluded that while some gaps existed that needed closing, there was not a case for the sweeping changes advocated by some in the defence and security community.

Research collaboration with China can also raise ethical concerns. For example, universities have faced allegations of working with Chinese partners on the development of technologies employed to repress China's Turkic Muslim ethnic minority in the far-western province of Xinjiang. Some universities have responded by reviewing and discontinuing collaborations when faced with such allegations, which suggests that these concerns may have some merit.

While scrutiny is valuable, in much public commentary it seems as if only collaborations involving China have ethical implications. Meanwhile, other partnerships, including with Western arms manufacturers, escape the same degree of scrutiny.

No one is suggesting that Australian universities should engage with China indiscriminately. But the overwhelming body of evidence points to robust engagement as firmly in the national interest, with the risks appropriately managed and balanced against the opportunities. And if curtailment might occasionally be needed, such decisions should be made on the basis of facts, not vague, overhyped "threats".

James Laurenceson is director of the Australia–China
Relations Institute at the University of Technology Sydney

Salvatore Babones

n 2018, international student numbers at Australian universities shot up 11 per cent – the biggest increase in more than a decade, according to Department of Education and Training data. Between 2013 and 2018, the numbers grew an astounding 46 per cent. And those are enrolment figures, meaning they mostly count students who are settled in their degrees. Course commencements presumably rose even faster.

But this trend is changing. Data for the 2018–2019 fiscal year show that new visa grants for higher education students rose only 6 per cent, and were absolutely flat for Chinese students, the most lucrative group. Chinese students generate particularly high fee revenue for universities because they tend to pay full fees and are concentrated in high-margin business master's programs.

In "High Price", Margaret Simons cautions that geopolitical risks could result in a sudden withdrawal of Chinese students from Australian universities. She also notes that a "slow decline" in Chinese student numbers is "almost certain" due to the rising quality of China's universities relative to Australia's. She's not wrong to warn about these factors. But she misses the bigger story.

As I wrote in August 2019, in a paper for the Centre for Independent Studies ("The China Student Boom and the Risks It Poses to Australian Universities"), the real risk is financial. When the Chinese yuan falls relative to the Australian dollar, the comparative price of an Australian degree increases. We saw this in the 2008–09 fiscal year, when the Aussie dollar shot up one-third almost overnight. Sure enough, enrolments collapsed, as Simons noted – but not, as she supposed, because of visa rule changes. Those rule changes may have hit the vocational education and training sector hard, but it was almost certainly the spike in the Australian dollar that drove away new university students.

The 2017 South Korean deployment of the American Terminal High Altitude Area Defense (THAAD) missile system is a key precedent for evaluating the effect that geopolitical developments can have on Australia-bound Chinese student numbers. In retaliation for Seoul's cooperation with Washington, Beijing put the kibosh on the sale of package tours to South Korea. But the data showed that Chinese student numbers in South Korea continued to grow. Similarly, repeated Chinese consular warnings about the treatment of Chinese students in Australia have had no reported effect on Australian universities' recruitment efforts.

It's politically difficult for the Chinese government to "weaponise" student flows because overseas study represents a long-term investment for hundreds of thousands of relatively well-to-do Chinese families. Dragging students home would provoke much more resistance than simply suspending the sale of holidays that haven't yet been booked anyway.

Similarly, the rising quality of Chinese universities is irrelevant to future student numbers in Australia. It's sad to say, but Chinese students don't come to Australia for the quality of its education. They come for the lifestyle, and because they can't get into top Chinese or American universities. Virtually no one who gets into Peking, Tsinghua or Fudan chooses Sydney, Melbourne or ANU instead. Australian universities aren't competing with Chinese ones; they're competing with British and Canadian ones.

Since 2017, it's the British who have been winning the Chinese recruitment game, and again, it's all down to currency movements. After the 2016 Brexit referendum, the Bank of England let the pound fall 10 per cent in value. That made UK universities effectively 10 per cent cheaper. While Russell Group vice-chancellors (the Russell Group includes twenty-four UK public research universities) crow that their stellar reputations are attracting record numbers of Chinese applicants, it's really all about their cut-rate prices.

You can't put a price on wisdom, but you can put a price on a university degree. Given how focused Australian vice-chancellors are on attracting Chinese student fee income, you'd think that they might reflect on how exchange rates affect the attractiveness of their offerings. But fond as they are of repeating the shibboleth that education is Australia's third export industry (which is only true if you cut and slice the definition of an "industry" just right), they never seem to want to admit that money matters to their customers – ahem, students.

With the Australian dollar currently trading at a ten-year low and the Chinese yuan only just starting to feel the effects of the US–China trade war, an Australian university degree still looks like a bargain when priced from China. If the Chinese economy collapses and the PRC suspends the convertibility of the yuan, look out. The Chinese student boom might go bust faster than anyone thinks.

Salvatore Babones is an adjunct scholar at the Centre for Independent Studies

---

Read more correspondence on Margaret Simons' "High Price" at www.australianforeignaffairs.com/articles

Margaret Simons responds

I am pleased James Laurenceson acknowledges that my article talks to Chinese students, not only about them. That was one of my aims. I get worried when current affairs programs depict Chinese students only as a threat. A *Four Corners* program last October, which showed Chinese students walking around campus while sinister music played in the background, made me fear for my students. They are young people to whom we owe a duty of care, not a homogeneous mass of foreign agents.

However, without getting into the separate but related issue of university research collaborations, I don't entirely share Laurenceson's exclusively sunny view of the Chinese student boom.

Some themes emerge strongly from my interactions with Chinese students. First, most have a conviction that this is China's time, and they are proud and excited about that – though some see a difference between love of country and love of the Chinese Communist Party.

They want to be part of the rise of their nation. That is natural enough. But when they think of their home country, there is a broad acceptance of the need for tight control, including around freedom of speech and of the press. They enjoy the freedoms Australia offers, but have little ambition to take these back with them. The common argument they offer is that China's large population and comparatively low education levels make tight social control necessary in the interests of harmony.

For example, while views differ on the Hong Kong protests, a clear majority seem to believe that they are the product of foreign interference and that the protesters are misguided. Many are distressed about the Australian media's reporting of the protests, and distrustful of it.

Generalisations are necessarily false, but I will chance my arm and say that we are not succeeding, as educators, in encouraging a critical re-evaluation of these views among our Chinese students. We are failing to sell the liberal ideals that underlie our system of education. The students too often move through their Australian education in a bubble, accessing only Chinese media and socialising only with their countryfolk.

This is a lost opportunity. But worse than that, it is a failure to truly educate.

Only a tiny minority of Chinese students are politically active – either for the Chinese Communist Party or in opposition to it. Nevertheless, at the moment, through force of numbers and the revenue they bring, the students are changing us more than we are changing them.

If we accept that our Western liberal system of education cannot get students to think critically and examine their assumptions, then our failure is deep indeed – and carries with it its own threat.

Turning to my other interlocutor, Salvatore Babones is heroic in attributing changes in the flow of student numbers to a single cause – exchange rates – and in attributing students' motivation to only two factors – lifestyle and an inability to get into top universities at home or in the United States. Those factors are of course in the mix, but Babones' analysis is too simplistic and, based on available data, too confident.

Of course it would be very difficult for China to suddenly stop the flow of students to Australia, but it would not be impossible, as Babones implies. For example, a new law prohibiting undergraduates from studying overseas would be a relatively simple matter – and easier to justify as China's own universities improve.

China, unlike Australia, is investing hugely in its tertiary sector. There are new universities springing up everywhere, and the older ones are expanding. Depending on which ranking you look at, there are now either four or five – including Fudan – in the top 100 in the world, and many more in the top 500. This is one of the reasons that relying on the revenue from international student business is risky for Australia – why this period is almost certainly a boom, rather than a sustainable business model.

When I worked at the University of Melbourne between 2011 and 2016,

I was sent on a number of marketing trips to China. I gave presentations in lecture halls where the walls above the hot water radiators were stained black from air pollution, and my throat stung whenever I went outside. I showed PowerPoint slides with views of the University of Melbourne campus, laid out under a crisp blue sky. This, as any Chinese student will tell you, is one of our selling points – clean air. A city that still has a blue sky? Almost unheard of.

The research tells us that another market advantage over the United States is a perception of safety. Mass shootings in America are well publicised in China. Another advantage is that we are closer to China than the United Kingdom and in a time zone that makes it easier to keep in touch with friends and family. Our visa system, which includes the chance to stay in Australia and work after graduation, is another drawcard.

The lectures I gave in China were on media and communications, including the place of journalism in a democracy. There was no obvious restriction on what I could talk about. I spoke freely, and nobody suggested I should not.

To be sure, I noticed a change over the five years of visits. Colleagues at Chinese universities told me they were having to be more careful about what they published and said in public. Meanwhile, the nightly banquets had been replaced by simple buffet meals of vegetables and rice. This, I was told, was part of President Xi Jinping's anti-corruption push. But, as one of my Chinese colleagues put it, "this is not the end of history". Xi will not last forever, and any sensible response to China should be able to contemplate what might follow his reign.

In the evenings of summer semester at Fudan, the university's gardens took on the look of a community park. People came out of the apartment buildings nearby and picnicked on the main lawn, under the gaze of a giant statute of Mao. The university embraced its community, and the students, most of whom lived in dormitories on campus, were in turn embraced.

It was above my pay scale to assess the success of the faculty's efforts to engage with China beyond the commodification of students, but if part of the purpose was to educate us academics, it worked for me. Simplistic views of what China is and might become do not survive such encounters. Nor do simplistic ideas of what it means for Australia's top universities to educate swathes of the emerging Chinese middle class, while charging them top dollar.

Meanwhile, wandering through university campuses, I became powerfully aware that China, too, is in the international education business. On the lawns under Mao's gaze, I met impressive students from Afghanistan and the developing nations of Africa. The best and brightest from the developing world are studying in China, with their fees and living expenses paid by the Chinese government. China is exporting its great promise – its unrivalled record in delivering millions of its own people from starvation in the course of just a generation – to the developing world.

While Australia makes money, China makes soft power.

Margaret Simons is a board member of the Public Interest Journalism Initiative

Subscribe to Australian Foreign Affairs & save up to 28% on the cover price.

Enjoy free home delivery of the print edition and full digital as well as ebook access to the journal via the Australian Foreign Affairs website, iPad, iPhone and Android apps.

Forthcoming issue:
Spy vs Spy
(July 2020)

Never miss an issue. Subscribe and save.

☐ **1 year auto-renewing print and digital subscription** (3 issues) $49.99 within Australia. Outside Australia $79.99*.

☐ **1 year print and digital subscription** (3 issues) $59.99 within Australia. Outside Australia $99.99.

☐ **1 year auto-renewing digital subscription** (3 issues) $29.99.*

☐ **2 year print and digital subscription** (6 issues) $114.99 within Australia.

☐ Tick here to commence subscription with the current issue.

Give an inspired gift. Subscribe a friend.

☐ **1 year print and digital gift subscription** (3 issues) $59.99 within Australia. Outside Australia $99.99.

☐ **1 year digital-only gift subscription** (3 issues) $29.99.

☐ **2 year print and digital gift subscription** (6 issues) $114.99 within Australia.

☐ Tick here to commence subscription with the current issue.

ALL PRICES INCLUDE GST, POSTAGE AND HANDLING.

*Your subscription will automatically renew until you notify us to stop. Prior to the end of your subscription period, we will send you a reminder notice.

Please turn over for subscription order form, or subscribe online at **australianforeignaffairs.com**
Alternatively, call 1800 077 514 or +61 3 9486 0288 or email **subscribe@australianforeignaffairs.com**

Back Issues

ALL PRICES INCLUDE GST, POSTAGE AND HANDLING.

- ☐ **AFA1** ($15.99)
  The Big Picture

- ☐ **AFA2** ($15.99)
  Trump in Asia

- ☐ **AFA3** ($15.99)
  Australia & Indonesia

- ☐ **AFA4** ($15.99)
  Defending Australia

- ☐ **AFA5** ($15.99)
  Are We Asian Yet?

- ☐ **AFA6** ($22.99)
  Our Sphere of Influence

- ☐ **AFA7** ($22.99)
  China Dependence

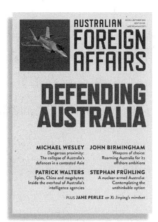

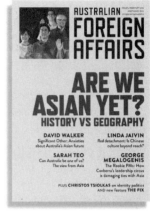

PAYMENT DETAILS I enclose a cheque/money order made out to Schwartz Books Pty Ltd. Or please debit my credit card (MasterCard, Visa or Amex accepted).

CARD NO. ☐☐☐☐ ☐☐☐☐ ☐☐☐☐ ☐☐☐☐

EXPIRY DATE   /   CCV   AMOUNT $

CARDHOLDER'S NAME

SIGNATURE

NAME

ADDRESS

EMAIL   PHONE

Post or fax this form to: Reply Paid 90094, Carlton VIC 3053 **Freecall:** 1800 077 514 **or** +61 3 9486 0288
Fax: (03) 9011 6106 **Email:** subscribe@australianforeignaffairs.com **Website:** australianforeignaffairs.com
Subscribe online at australianforeignaffairs.com/subscribe (please do not send electronic scans of this form)

AFA WEEKLY

OUR WORLD IN DEPTH

A **free** weekly email from Australian Foreign Affairs journal

SUBSCRIBE TODAY

AUSTRALIANFOREIGNAFFAIRS.COM/AFA-WEEKLY

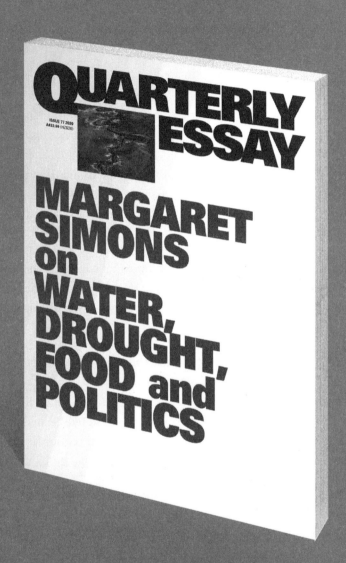

The Back Page

STOCHASTIC TERRORISM

What is it: The use of mass communication to incite individual, unpredictable acts of terrorism. Examples commonly cited are the assassinations of Yitzhak Rabin (former prime minister, Israel) and Jo Cox (former anti-Brexit Labour MP, United Kingdom). "Stochastic", a word borrowed from mathematics, refers to processes that are random, so can be analysed statistically but not predicted.

When did it take hold: In August 2019, after a mass shooting by a white nationalist in El Paso, Texas, dictionary.com reported a 63,389 per cent surge in searches for the term. Prominent agitators described as stochastic terrorists include Alex Jones (publisher, InfoWars) and Donald Trump (president, United States), who said gun-rights activists might "do" something if Hillary Clinton won the 2016 election.

Who coined it: Unexpectedly, an insurance consultant. Gordon Woo (catastrophist, Risk Management Solutions), used the term in a paper, suggesting terrorism events could be modelled using economic principles. Emily Bell (professor, Columbia Journalism School) noted: "Where there is a saturation of inflammatory rhetoric about ideology or particular groups … it becomes statistically likely that some lone wolf will take the bait."

Have we seen it before: Yes. Ulius Louis Amoss (former intelligence officer, CIA) outlined "leaderless resistance" to communism in the 1950s. White supremacist groups adapted this into the figure of the "lone wolf" terrorist.

Can it be stopped: Woo quotes Philip Roth (deceased literary icon, United States) on history: "Everything unexpected in its own time is chronicled on the page as inevitable. The terror of the unforeseen is what the science of history hides."